CW00401448

The Final Great Path

By the same author

The Final Great Path – Kindle edition (includes both East & West)
The Final Great Path – West

THE FINAL GREAT PATH

EAST

James Montague Bedford-Stradling, Ph.D.

James Montague Bedford-Stradling

Copyright© 2020 James Bedford-Stradling

All rights reserved

DEDICATION

A heartfelt thanks and appreciation: To all the saints and sages, past and present, who have safeguarded the sacred teachings of both east and west, many at great risk to themselves, many who have suffered persecution and even paid the ultimate price with their lives. Without these brave souls this knowledge would have been lost forever.

To historians who have painstakingly researched and tabulated the various disciplines of spiritual and religious subject matter worldwide. My love and heartfelt eternal gratitude to my ultimate martial mentor, Tenth Degree Professor David Lyons, whose martial school of Zenyogkido (The Way of Mind, Body and Spirit), is firmly founded on ancient spiritual traditions. His system made spirituality a living reality; not just a part time intellectual exercise.

A special mention has to go to my closest of mere mortal men, Peter D Smith. We have travelled this very difficult path together, sharing our trials and tribulations along with some incredible adventures. Without his undying love, friendship and support I would have fallen from the path a long time ago – much love to you my brother.

Finally, to Deus, mere words cannot express my eternal love and gratitude to this most amazing of incarnated life forms; far beyond just human. His personal teachings actually delivered the very meaning of life – something I craved and sought, after watching my father pass away. Deus was/is the embodiment of the ultimate power of creation and the universe... LOVE.

James Montague Bedford-Stradling

TABLE OF CONTENTS

FOREWORD

My search for spiritual truth encompassed a multitude of traditions from around the world spanning well over three decades. It has ranged from orthodox religions and the western mystery traditions to the various yogic scriptures of India. It has long been my intention to make accessible the outcome of my search, study and application. Here is the first book of two, The Final Great Path – *East.* The second is The Final Great Path – *West.*

This first book deals with the teaching given by a secret hidden master. The second deals with the hidden and very secretive teachings, spanning thousands of years, by underground secret societies of the west.

For many decades now, the yogic tradition of the east has become accessible to the world in general, although still very much misunderstood by the masses.

However, what I know to be unique about these two books, is that the spiritual content and teaching presented draws together that of the eastern, western secret and orthodox spiritual traditions.

Although east and west express the path in very different language, you will find that the central message and goal is exactly the same. The thing that draws together all of these paths and lends truth to what is presented here, is the Great Pyramid of Gizeh. This is, unbeknown to the masses, the foundation for the secret western tradition. The Great Pyramid's encrypted spiritual teaching, purpose and truth is explained in the second book; the Final Great Path - *West.*

Here I would just like to put the mind at rest for the reader who is already following a faith. These two books are not intended to replace any faith or religion, rather they are intended to enrich your own faith.

These two books are also aimed at those who at present are not actively engaged with any particular faith, and who may be searching for answers, or looking for direction. The most debilitating and crippling aspect to the human condition is the loss of purpose; that ineffable question; what is the meaning of life? Hopefully you will find what you have been looking for within these pages and wake each morning with a real purpose to your existence.

Within these pages you will find the ancient teachings, as delivered by a hidden master. His beautiful teachings, congruent to the message of the Great Pyramid of Gizeh, speaks for itself.

The main objective of these two books then, is to bring together what in the past has been divided and scattered over the course of time and deliver the actual unified core spiritual message. In the Judaic and Christian traditions, it is the return to the Garden of Eden.

For humanity in general, whatever the language, this means striving to regain our Divine spiritual inheritance.

So, here in The Final Great Path – East, you will find a clear and concise guide, it covers most areas of spirituality and instructs the aspirant how to incorporate spirituality into their daily lives; without the need for showmanship or the need to escape everyday life.

PRELUDE

My father, who was in a coma on his death bed, was being read his last rights by the Roman Catholic Priest. As I held my father's hand the priest tried to push the wafer of last Holy Communion into his dried out mouth; the same mouth that I had been trying to keep moist over the past few days with saline swabs. Startling us all, my father suddenly sat bolt upright in his bed and pushed the unwanted hand away from his mouth.

With all of his senses miraculously restored my father exclaimed, 'What's going on?'

My mother tried to reassure him. 'It's ok Paddy it's only the priest, just try to lay down.'

'But what's it all been about? Why are we here? The time has gone so quickly.' Dad replied.

I sat there holding my father's hand as he laid back down, slipping back into a coma that he wouldn't return from. Barely able to choke back the tears, in that moment I knew my mission in life.

I swore to search and find the spiritual truth no matter what, even if it took me until my dying day. Even if I hadn't found the elusive "meaning of life" – then at least I could say to myself. *This life has been worthwhile for at least I have tried.*

Different things can be read in to what my father said, but for me it was quite clear; his time on earth had gone too quickly and he was asking what the point of life was all about. The system hadn't prepared him for the end; in fact the system didn't have any answers to the human condition at all. I decided at that point that no matter what, I would search for the reason as to why we are here; this oath led me to my ultimate teacher.

There is one statement that my Master made that is never far from the forefront of my mind – it is one heck of a powerful statement.

'James, there are two points of reference in this life, dying and waiting to die, what you do in between is up to you.'

Like many who try to search out the mystery of life, I found the bewildering amount of paths proclaiming "This is the way!" totally confusing. I was led into the western mystery tradition such as the world of Kabbalah, Mysticism, Astrology and the esoteric. I studied the works of The Golden Dawn, Freemasonry, Rosicrucian's and many more such secret societies. I used comparative Religion as a touch stone to ensure I would remain firmly grounded. I was looking for the common denominator that would lead me to the heart of life's mystery

While investigating Buddhism; I became a member of the FWBO (Friends of the Western Buddhist Order), and was taught meditation by a Monk called Guhya-Ratna, which translates as Hidden Gem within the Lotus.

I attended spiritual retreats in the hills of Shropshire and the mountains of North Wales, some of these solitary, although I eventually moved away from the Buddhist path. From here I took up Ha-Tha Yoga; Rajah Yoga; Jnana Yoga and Karma Yoga.

During my search for truth I became interested in the Great Pyramid of Gizeh. I didn't believe that this awesome monument was built purely as a tomb for an ancient King, I had a gut feeling that such a huge project must have been undertaken to convey a message or a teaching for humanity. You see the clue is in this awesome monument's ancient Egyptian name, Ta-Khut, meaning "The Light".

It was a moment of inspiration/revelation in the interpretation of the Great Pyramid of Gizeh that cleared the fog of spiritual confusion, I knew beyond doubt that the reason for human incarnation is to tread the spiritual path of transcendental transformation.

Linking this fervent search for truth must be self-discipline; this focus on self-discipline would actually lead me, in the most unsuspecting manner, to my ultimate teacher.

I took up a martial art called Zenyogkido (The Way of the Mind, Body and Spirit), which as the name suggests is a holistic system, unlike most martial schools in the west. The spiritual, meditative side to this martial school has no allegiance to any particular religion, it rises above all dogma.

The founder bestowed the great honour upon me of Grand Master (and co-regent with my closest friend Pete), of this all-encompassing system.

I met my closest friend, Grand Master Peter Smith, in 1994 when he walked into St Guthlac' Hall, the venue for the Kung Fu martial art of Zenyogkido.

We have trained consistently together for over two decades in Zenyogkido. This martial connection was/is the foundation for our friendship, a shared passion if you will.

There is however, outside of the martial connection, something far more profound and totally unique about our amazing friendship. Through the founder of Zenyogkido the two of us would meet and become devotees of a hidden spiritual master, but not just any ordinary human Master/Guru, we suspected him of being an Avatar. A far deeper look into precisely what an Avatar is and how an Avatar works, will be covered shortly.

I mention this here prior to the section on Avatars for good reason; as this was the beginning of a lifetime friendship and shared experiences.

From then on our life's journey has been inseparable, but not only inseparable, after only a few years of friendship, we realised that we were leading parallel lives – whatever Pete was going through it seemed I was going through, whatever I would be going through, Pete was going through the same...it was and still is quite inexplicable.

Over the next few decades, when I was spiritually down Pete would pick me up and when Pete was down I would return the favour. Countless times we would find ourselves moaning (ego selves), about our apparent lack of progress, and yet this would always find a balance in our chats about amazing situations and experiences.

In fact, more or less right from the onset of our dedication to the master, he stated to us both, 'You must stick together, for neither of you are strong enough to walk this path alone.'

The factors that came together in meeting the master were not pure luck, for as you will discover within these pages, nothing happens by accident. I had been gently picked up by the one who became my teacher, he dusted me down with tender love and care and unravelled the tangled mess, slowly undid the Gordian knot of my environmental conditioning. But the main point is...all was achieved by taking little steps over a long period of time; I will never be able to thank my ultimate mentor enough.

THE FINAL GREAT PATH

PART ONE

THE FRIEND OF GOD

CHAPTER 1

AVATARS

The concept/reality of an Avatar holds that God has incarnated in a human body, a reality far more readily acceptable to the Hindu faith than most other faiths. The Hindu faith is the oldest religion in the world, having its origin in the Indus valley. Most scholars date the Vedas to c. 2000 BCE and although contentious, some believe these sacred texts of the Hindu Vedas may date as far back as 4,000 BCE.

Echoes of this same belief in Avatars can be heard in Buddhism with the incarnation of Bodhisattvas; an enlightened being who has decided, through compassion, to reincarnate in order to help struggling humanity.

I say echoes of this belief as Buddhism, which derived from Hinduism, does not have a belief in God. Oddly enough it is well recorded that the Hindu God, Brahma, in the aspect of the creator, appeared before Buddha to ask him to teach humanity what he had discovered.

Here we will have a closer look at the better known Avatars. I must admit that to begin with I had great difficulty with this subject; God walking the Earth, not just in one body but plural. However, taking the assertion of Christianity that Jesus was/is the son of God helped me wrestle with this stand point. Not only that, who am I to say what God can and cannot do, after all God is God and can do whatever God wants to do? There is a real need here for the reader, no matter what faith you may subscribe to, or indeed no faith whatsoever, to have an open mind.

There is one common denominator between all major faiths…God; that energy that is everything, that unifies everything and everyone…a power that can manifest in what appears to be multiplicity but in fact is one unity.

Fundamentally we cannot quantify or qualify God with our limited human mind; our five senses and intellect are severely limited.

So in Hinduism Lord Krishna is an Avatar, and by the same definition Lord Jesus is an Avatar and is recognised as such in the yogic traditions of India. It is also becoming widely accepted in ever increasing circles that the Virgin Mother Mary is an Avatar.

Incarnated into the 20th/21st century are three other Avatars, Shri Shirdi Sai Baba; Shri Sathya Sai Baba and Mother Meera. It is pertinent to pre-empt a certain question here, *Why so many Avatars in recent history?* The answer to this question is quite simple, God incarnates in human form as an Avatar to communicate directly when humanity is in crisis.

All of these incarnations about to be related, happen to coincide with what the Hindu tradition calls the Kali Yuga, or the ultimate age of darkness. Krishna, who lived for something like one hundred and twenty-five years, departed this world once his work had been accomplished. Krishna's departure was right on the cusp of the beginning of the Dark Age, Mother Mary and Jesus incarnated in the middle and Shirdi and Sathya Sai Baba along with Divine Mother Meera at the end; right on the cusp of the Treta Yuga, the age of Truth. This Avatar intensity at the end of the Kali Yuga is to usher in the start of the Golden Age. However, the human race must make a major effort to realign their focus and aspiration toward the Divine; God will help but won't do everything.

Each Avatar can be considered as one facet of a diamond and yet at the same time the whole diamond. What we see is the one facet, but the whole diamond is behind it and around it. Another way of looking at this reality is to consider a crystal lamp shade, this lamp shade is divided into sections each having its own colour, and yet the light within the shade is the one internal light that shines through each coloured segment.

Each Avatar adopts their own unique approach and mechanisms in different locations and epochs. The sole aim of each Avatar is for the dispersal of ignorance and the lifting of human consciousness.

These approaches impact upon the human mind in many and varied ways according to the culture of the time. If the tongue is only accustomed to a bland pallet – hot spices are introduced to shock and jolt the tongue and mind. If the eyes are only used to the twilight, the brilliant spectre of the sunrise is introduced and if the ears are only used to a humdrum drone, exquisite heavenly music is orchestrated.

This is the impact, pre-designed by each Avatar, according to the needs of the time...so designed to make the children (humanity), sit up and take notice.

Here we will have a very brief look at each coloured light, each colour representing an incarnation of an Avatar. The first of the five best known Avatars is Lord Krishna.

Lord Krishna

'Offer all thy works to God.'

Sri Krishna was born in northern India in approximately 3,228 BCE. The sacred texts of the Puranas consider Sri Krishna's life to mark the passing of the Dvapara Yuga in to the Kali Yuga.

Krishna was born in prison to devout parents – Devaki and Vasudeva. At the time of his birth, his life was in danger because the tyrant Kamsa was seeking to kill him; this story is echoed in the circumstances of the birth of both Moses and Jesus.

It had been foretold that Kamsa would be killed by Devaki's eighth child. Since Sri Krishna was the eighth child, he was smuggled out of prison to be raised by his foster parents Nanda and Yasoda in Gokula. Nanda lived a simple lifestyle and was a chief in the local Cow-herding community. The young Sri Krishna is often depicted in these days as being a mischievous child, who enjoyed playing pranks and having fun. Many devotees of Krishna worship him in his innocent childhood aspect.

This aspect of Krishna in childhood, his innocence and spontaneous mischievousness is very important regarding the message of most, if not all Avatars. The Avatar Lord Jesus stated, 'Unless you become as little children you cannot enter the kingdom of heaven.' Mother Meera states much the same quality needed for walking the spiritual path and that a self-realised person has the qualities of a child. And of course all Avatars state that we are all children of the Divine. It would seem that we as so-called adult humans, take ourselves far too seriously, and therefore lack humility.

With regards to becoming like little children, I always had difficulty in trying to comprehend as to how and in what manner. Yes I get the thing about becoming spontaneous, but as an adult that in itself is pretty difficult. This particular day I was as usual hosting the meditation group, this question had been on my mind, regarding the child bit, for some time. Prior to the meditation I always have a chat with the group relating to our spiritual practice. This day I talked about weaving the Divine within our normal daily activities – fundamentally a kind of mindfulness practice that focuses on our true source. Anyway, now deep in meditation at some point a kind of parable presented itself to the mind:

In this world be as a little child that has become lost, a child that is crying, searching and yearning for its mother or father.

One day, a lost child in much distress sees its mother standing upon a hill, at that moment of jubilation the child runs as fast as it can to its mother. The mother who has been searching frantically for the lost child, rushes towards the infant; the two come together in an embrace of pure love where tears of joy are shed...the child has finally come home.

Adopt this focus in heart and mind and incorporate it within your meditation as well.

Returning to normal human consciousness from the meditation, eyes moist from this epiphany, the story was related to the group. What made this parable particularly poignant was that shortly after this entering the mind, I heard the rapid running footsteps and excited voices of children running up the corridor just outside the closed door of the meditation room; unusual as the room is a conference facility in a business centre.

As Krishna matured a deep love developed between him and Radha; Radha as his greatest devotee was deeply in love with Sri Krishna and as Krishna had stated himself in relation to the path of Bhakti Yoga, love of the Divine, that this love is reciprocated to any devotee. So Radha as his greatest devotee received the greatest love from Krishna. A similar theme is echoed in a Christian gnostic gospel, which relates how Jesus's closest disciple was Mary Magdalene. It is important here not to mistake human carnal love with Divine love; this Divine love cannot be expressed in human words.

Krishna was also very fond of the female gopis (cowherds), who were also devoted to him and would frequently be found playing his flute for them. There is one fable that actually gives the symbolic significance of his flute. Krishna asked a number of his devotees that, if given a choice, which of his symbols they would like to be. All chose various symbols of Vishnu, the highest aspect of Godhead that Krishna had incarnated from. Each stated these same symbols of Lotus flower, Mace, Conch Shell or Chakra/Solar disc. Krishna lamented the fact that none had said his flute and continued to relate that his flute symbolised the devotee who had surrendered to him (giving up ego), and that it would be him expressing Divine music through them.

Sri Krishna, considered to be the greatest of Avatars and ultimate personality of God, taught that there were many paths to reach the goal of self-realisation, but devotion was the shortest and safest path.

Bhagavad Gita: Chapter 4, verse 11. *'However men try to reach me, I return their love with my love; whatever path they may travel, it leads to me in the end.'*

Sri Krishna said to Arjuna in the opening section of the Bhagavad Gita: *'Whenever, O descendant of Bharata, righteousness declines and unrighteousness prevails, I manifest Myself.*

For the protection of the good and the destruction of the wicked, and for the establishment of righteousness, I come into being from age to age.'

This then brings me to the pinnacle of Sri Krishna's incarnation as recorded in the Bhagavad Gita, the central core of the epic Mahabharata. The Bhagavad Gita relates the story of Krishna's dialogue with his friend Arjuna, the prince of Pandava. On the eve of the great battle of Kurukshetra, Arjuna was having grave misgivings about engaging the enemy, comprising many of his relatives.

It was on the battlefield of Kurukshetra that Sri Krishna gave the Divine discourse of the Bhagavad Gita, which was an exposition of Sri Krishna's yoga and how an aspiring seeker should seek union with God. Unlike previous Indian scriptures, the Bhagavad Gita did not require escape from the world but encouraged world acceptance. The Bhagavad Gita and the life of Sri Krishna were very important for making spirituality accessible to ordinary people – and not just yogi's who renounced the world. The central message of Sri Krishna was for humanity to take part in the Divine cosmic dance or play (Lila in Hinduism), here on Earth, without expectation of reward and devoid of ego.

Bhagavad Gita Chapter 2, Verse 47. *'You are only entitled to the action, never to its fruits. Do not let the fruits of action be your motive, but do not attach yourself to non-action.'*

Krishna is accredited with many miracles, as are all Avatars, as a child he is said to have lifted a nearby hill, Govardhana, to protect the villagers against the wrath of the Goddess Indra which would have brought a huge flood upon the village.

Another anecdote has the child Krishna playing in the garden when his guardian observed him putting dirt in his mouth. His guardian ran out and questioned him as to why he had just eaten the soil. Krishna denied he had done such a thing but was asked to open his mouth. On doing so his guardian, in astonishment, observed the planets and universe therein.

This last story is quite profound, in as much as it came thousands of years before the scientific discovery of atoms – it would seem that here we have an analogy of atomic physics, in that the dirt is comprised of the same material as the universe.

One of the best-known miracles was on the battlefield of Kurukshetra. With the battle over Krishna brought the chariot to a halt; at this point Arjuna refused to disembark as it was traditional for the driver/charioteer to disembark first. However, Krishna held fast and would not go first, reluctantly Arjuna stepped down. Once Arjuna was safe on terra-firma Krishna disembarked; as soon as Krishna alighted the chariot burst into flames. During the battle the chariot had been hit by many flaming arrows, but Krishna had prevented them, temporarily, from combusting. So if Krishna had got off first Arjuna would have been consumed in the flames.

The beauty of the Bhagavad Gita is that it actually gives methodology to attain to the ever elusive "meaning of life". However, I must state here a certain confusion inherent within the text of this amazing little book, that Krishna states that all paths eventually lead to him, which of course they verily do.

Krishna mentions various types of yoga, Jnana Yoga; Karma Yoga etc. and of course the ultimate path of Bhakti Yoga. The reality and fact is, that all paths eventually lead to Bhakti Yoga, devotion to the Divine. Take for example Jnana Yoga, the yoga of knowledge, this knowledge eventually leads to Karma Yoga, that of right action. The Yoga of right action leads to Raja Yoga, that of right mental and emotional processes. This ultimately leads to Bhakti Yoga, the focus of the whole heart and mind upon the Divine; an edict that Moses pronounced and happens to be the message encrypted within the Great Pyramid.

The compilation of these various paths can be expressed as, *Right Knowledge, Right Conduct and Right Belief,* with the latter of right belief expressed by, *Focus, Affirmation and Aspiration,* the details of which you will encounter in due course.

It really doesn't matter from which point you start, whether Bhakti, Raja, Karma or Jnana Yoga, for each of the due processes eventually incorporate the other disciplines.

Sri Chinmoy, in his commentary on the Bhagavad Gita states, 'He [Krishna] brought down to the earth-consciousness the supreme Truth that earth and earthly life, being inherently Divine, must be made outwardly Divine, fully and totally, in every sphere, in every aspect.'

Regarding the Bhagavad Gita, there is another less well-known discourse from Krishna as recorded in the Puranas, the Uddhava Gita. The dialogue between Uddhava and Krishna took place just before Krishna departed this world; it is said to be the last teaching of Krishna. The difference between the two Gita' is that the first is dealing with the young warrior prince Arjuna, the friend of Krishna.

Primarily in this dialogue Krishna's answers are short pithy statements. However, with Uddhava we are dealing with a very much older and wiser man, not only a friend but a long term devotee of Krishna's; so Krishna's commentaries are in far greater detail as to the path we should be following.

Sai Baba of Shirdi

'Blessed is he who has become one with Me.'

Sai Baba of Shirdi was born in the mid-19th Century and departed this world in 1918. He was revered by both Hindus and Muslims alike. Sai lived in Shirdi all his life and was buried in the Buty Wada.

Sai Baba of Shirdi taught that all religions led to the same goal and sought to show the underlying unity between the Muslim and Hindu faiths. One of his most famous sayings was "God is the owner of us All"

Sai left no written records, however there is a strong oral legacy of teachings and parables that have been written down by his disciples. Sai made eleven assurances to his devotees:

1. Whosoever puts their feet on Shirdi soil, their sufferings will come to an end
2. The wretched and miserable will rise to joy and happiness as soon as they climb the steps of the mosque
3. I shall be ever active and vigorous even after leaving this earthly body
4. My tomb shall bless and speak to the needs of my devotees
5. I shall be active and vigorous even from my tomb
6. My mortal remains will speak from my tomb
7. I am ever living to help and guide all who come to me, who surrender to me and who seek refuge in me
8. If you look to me, I look to you
9. If you cast your burden on me, I shall surely bear it
10. If you seek my advice and help, it shall be given to you at once
11. There shall be no want in the house of my devotee

With regards to Baba's tomb, the Avatar Mother Meera states that the ground where an enlightened human is buried is sacred and blessed; how much more then for an Avatar? Like Jesus not much is known about his early life. It is believed

21

that he was brought up in the village of Pathri by a fakir and his wife. When Sai Baba was sixteen years old he arrived in the village of Shirdi in Maharashtra. He lived a very ascetic life, spending many hours immersed in meditation in a Khabdoba temple and later a dilapidated mosque. Without any preaching or attempt to attract followers, people were drawn to his presence, attracting followers of both the Hindu and Muslim faith. Sai could be a stern spiritual teacher when telling his disciples to shake their egoistic views. Some of His most well-known sayings are:

1. No harm shall befall him who sets his foot on the soil of Shirdi
2. He who cometh to My Samadhi, his sorrow and suffering shall cease
3. Though I be no more in flesh and blood, I shall ever protect My devotees
4. Trust in Me and your prayer shall be answered
5. Know that My Spirit is immortal. Know this for yourself
6. Show unto Me he who sought refuge and been turned away
7. In whatever faith men worship Me, even so do I render to them
8. Not in vain is My Promise that I shall ever lighten your burden
9. Knock, and the door shall open. Ask and ye shall be granted
10. To him who surrenders unto Me totally I shall be ever indebted
11. Blessed is he who has become one with Me

One of Sai's favourite teachings is the omnipresence of God – 'Why do you fear, when I am always here. He has no beginning and no end.'

A unique aspect to Shirdi Sai Baba is that he kept a sacred fire burning around the clock, the ash of this sacred fire, called Vibhutti, he would distribute to both visitors and followers alike. Many claimed that this sacred ash had miraculous attributes. Shirdi Sai Baba was also known for his ability to create spontaneous miracles, such as materialising objects out of thin air.

Now then, here we get onto that which is totally unfathomable regarding Sri Shirdi Sai Baba, not that the proceeding is anything other than unfathomable anyway. Shirdi Sai Baba stated that he was the first of three successive incarnations of God and that his next incarnation would be Sri Sathya Sai Baba. Shirdi Sai Baba even went as far as producing an image of his next incarnation, a slightly built orange robed figure with what can only be described as an afro hairstyle similar to that of Michael Jackson in his younger years.

In due course, Sri Sathya Sai Baba incarnated as the reincarnation of Sri Shirdi Sai Baba. One of Sri Sathya Sai Baba's favourite sayings was identical to Shirdi Sai Baba, "Why Fear when I am here." Sathya Sai Baba, just like Shirdi Sai Baba, is famous for his miraculous materialisation of trinkets from nowhere and unlike

Shirdi Sai Baba who physically distributed sacred ash from his fire, would manifest the sacred ash, Vibhutti, out of thin air.

Another miraculous phenomena relating to this Vibhutti, is that the sacred ash would spontaneously manifest from both Shirdi and Sathya Sai Baba's pictures, a miracle I have personally witnessed.

The following short biography of Sri Sathya Sai Baba, Shirdi Sai Baba's second of three incarnations, is reproduced with kind permission from my friend Pete's account of Avatars.

Sri Sathya Sai Baba

'Love all, Serve all.'

Without doubt the most prominent figure recently is Sathya Sai Baba. He was born Sathya Narayana Raju, in the state of Andhra Pradesh in the village of Puttaparthi in India on November the 23rd 1926. He was born to a poor agrarian family, as the son of Pedavenkappa Raju and Easwaramma. Being born after the Sri Sathyanarayana Puja, the child was consequently named after the puja's presiding deity, Sathyanarayana. It was reported that when he was born, musical instruments in the household started playing music on their own.

Sathya Sai Baba was a child prodigy, he composed bhajans (devotional songs) spontaneously. The simple village folk marvelled at the child's gifts, calling him Biddalaguru (child guru) and Brahmajnani (knowing universal truths). There were other qualities too in the child that captivated people — his sunny temperament, generous and loving nature and kindness to creatures great and small.

Even as a child Sathya was already manifesting extraordinary powers — plucking things out of the thin air, on one occasion even transfixing a scolding teacher to his chair. The smiling, frizzy-haired lad was half-prankster and half-conjurer in his schoolmates' eyes. He was bright, showing flair not only for academics, but also music, dance and drama.

On May 23rd 1940, when he was thirteen, after a two month period of illness and unconsciousness, Sathya Sai Baba declared to his parents and the villagers that he is an Avatar and had come to this world with a mission to re-establish the principle of righteousness, to motivate love for God and service to fellow man. He said that this was his second incarnation and claimed to be the reincarnation of the Muslim fakir Shirdi Sai Baba, a man who had passed away 8 years before Sathya was born, and subsequently he took the fakir's name. He proclaimed that he is an Avatar (incarnation) of Shiva and Shakti and an embodiment of love with divine powers such as omniscience and omnipresence. He then announced that there would be a third incarnation to come who would be known as Prema (love) Sai Baba and just like Shirdi he even created an image of what his third and last incarnation would look like; Prema Sai Baba's image is strikingly like that of Jesus the Christ. Over these three lives his mission is to bring the religions of the world together as one brotherhood/sisterhood with universal love as their foundation stone.

After this announcement, he quickly became recognised by many to be a holy man and over the course of his life he has done so many amazing things that the catalogue of experiences is too vast to record. I will outline a few of the stories of Sri Sathya Sai Baba's miracles to give you a taste of the man's incredible abilities and presence.

The first story and one of the most often told is that of the now former proprietor of the Hard Rock Café restaurant chain in America; Isaac Tigrett.

Tigrett was driving his Porsche along the Malibu hills by the sea at around 90 miles an hour, when it careered over the edge and plunged down a 300ft drop. In Tigrett's description of the event, as he plunged over the cliff a man in orange robes with a mop of fuzzy hair appeared beside him in the car and put his arms around him. The car crashed to a shuddering and devastating halt at the bottom of the cliff totally destroyed, with the sea's waves crashing over it. However, Tigrett emerged without even a bruise. Following this, Tigrett went to see Baba and although being refused an audience numerous times before, was given a personal meeting with him. During the audience, to Tigrett's utter amazement, unprompted, Baba suddenly started talking to Tigrett about the crash, describing it to him in detail and reminding him that Baba had been there with him and had saved him.

Baba then explained to Tigrett that he had saved him for a purpose, and simply asked him to sell his interests in the Hard Rock café chain, to build a hospital in India, which would be free to all. Then to his disbelief he told Tigrett it would need to be completed in a year.

As you can imagine for most people this would be an enormous test for the ego. I know if someone asked me to sell my home and donate the proceeds to a charity, I would be asking myself if I was being conned. Mr Tigrett though, promptly sold his chain under the condition that the new owners display the Baba universal statement of "Love all Serve All" as a corporate slogan to be used on all the literature and signage.

Once sold Tigrett donated the 16 million dollars from the sale to become the principal sponsor of the creation of the Sri Sathya Sai Institute of Higher Medicine, a free 500-bed advanced surgical hospital that serves the rural poor in Anantapur,

India. As if that wasn`t amazing enough, the project did actually open a year later. Obviously, the experience of Sai Baba saving his life in the car crash was an undeniable affirmation of Baba`s divinity for Tigrett.

As it turns out though, this was not the only time that Baba saved his life as Tigrett himself describes in another interview.

'I had an epileptic fit and swallowed my tongue and died on the floor of this hotel room thereby missing my flight connections. Suddenly this guru, who I had been following for two years, named Sri Sathya Sai Baba, appeared in the room. My spirit came out of the top of my head and I was in some sort of form of giddy electricity, conscious of myself and of my separateness from my dead body, which was lying ten feet below me. Sai Baba picked me up, put me on a bed, pulled my tongue out, pressed on my chest-and my spirit went back inside my body. I looked up and there he was smiling at me.'

Although, unlike in the case above, Sai Baba doesn`t ask for money from his devotees, nevertheless he is given a great deal of money from them in the form of donations. The majority of these he invested in the running of his two free hospitals and into schemes to help the poor and needy, such as supplying water and basic human needs to poorer villages.

He has also set upon the task of providing profound education programmes with a strong moral base, opening many schools and universities. Baba believes that education taught without a strong moral base is wasted. The human being, he says, needs a holistic education, one that includes values.

Baba's universal message extended to phenomena directed to the Roman Catholic faith. On his deathbed, Pope John XXIII is said to have had a vision of a man that would usher in a new Golden Age such as mankind has never known. He described him as a small, barefooted man with brown skin who will wear a distinctive orange/red robe. Similarly, the great 16th century seer Nostradamus and American prophet Edgar Cayce predicted that a holy man from the east would challenge the major religions of the world as a prelude to a Golden Age. Baba is that being.

Oddly, as I write now, on a personal note, I remember as a sixth former rushing to get the latest weekly copy of "Punch", an intellectual humorous magazine, and reading it , whilst laughing out loud in the common room at the columns and cartoons it contained. This is the part that is odd, years later, there is only one thing I can remember from the hundreds of "Punch" magazines I consumed in those days and it is a cartoon.

The setting was in heaven, with clouds and a big throne. In front of the throne are two Angels sitting and talking to each other. Slumped on the throne, wearing only a tattered loin cloth, is a small pot-bellied scraggly man with a mane of unkempt crazy hair. Underneath the punchline, (which is one of the angels whispering to the other), reads: `Frankly I`m quite disappointed!`

The joke, which I laughed about for ages, is that how could God be anything less than magnificent in every way.

The thing with Sai baba is, he's not what you'd expect a God man to look like. He is a small man with a distinctive sometimes unruly mop of black fuzzy hair similar to the style popularised by the young Michael Jackson in the 70`s. And just like the deathbed vision of the coming saviour described by Pope John XXIII he is barefooted and wears an orange/red robe.

Yet despite this, many world leaders rank amongst his followers, including the onetime president and prime minister of India S D Sharma and P V Narasimha Rao, as well as the ex-prime ministers of Italy and Norway. The Duchess of York (Fergie) has been to see him and rumour has it that Prince Charles requested an audience but was refused. In India Sai Baba is headline news and his influence is rapidly spreading to the West.

Never before has anyone displayed such remarkable powers. The reports coming out of India are mind boggling. Sai Baba has raised the dead, multiplied food as Christ did, materialises jewellery out of the air and turned water into petrol when his car ran out of fuel.

There are tales of him materialising sweets directly into people's mouths, appearing in two places at once and making a photograph of the face of Christ appear on film. Most of his manifestations have been demonstrated in front of highly respected professional people and are particularly well documented by Dr John Hislop and Howard Murphet.

Amongst the "Sai Stories" told by devotees are some very strange anecdotes. For example: Knowing that every Rolex watch has its exclusive serial number, an Australian visitor asked the swami to materialise one for him. Sai Baba obliged with a wave of his hand. On his return the serial number enabled the Australian to identify where the watch had been purchased. He asked the proprietor if he remembered who bought it. The owner remembered the occasion well. He could hardly forget the unusual orange clad Indian`gentleman with strange fuzzy hair.

The shop owner was a meticulous man who kept accurate sales records that gave not only the day of purchase but the time as well. Together they checked the records. It corresponded exactly with the time and day that Sai Baba had materialised the Rolex. Sai Baba had been in two places at the same time.

Another intriguing story, although accounts differ, concerns an Australian who visited Sai Baba in the hope that he could cure his wife of terminal cancer. Sai Baba spoke to him saying `You shouldn't be here. Your wife needs you. She will be well.' He then tapped the Australian three times on the forehead. The man vanished in front of a crowd of people and reappeared besides his wife's hospital bed in Australia. Baffled by what happened he checked his passport. It was stamped correctly with that day's date yet only moments ago he was in India. His wife recovered.

All over the world there are people who have had similar impossible experiences. Sai Baba's most frequent materialisation is of a healing ash called Vibhutti. Hindus consider this to be very holy and on a par with the holy sacrament of Christianity.

In the Daily Telegraph of 6th March 1992 a reporter witnessed Vibhutti ash forming on photos of Sai Baba and objects in the room at the home of Mr G Patel in Wealdstone, Harrow, London. In honour of Sai Baba's 70th Birthday, Mr Patel carved a life-size wooden statue of his guru. As soon as the task was complete Vibhutti ash began to form on the statue's hands, gown and feet. Mr Patel took a photograph of this but when the film was developed it was not the statue in the picture but a photograph of the real Sri Sathya Sai Baba.

He is said to manifest this Vibhutti and other small objects like rings and watches daily. He claims to materialize these objects out of nothing. These claims are believed and testified to by his followers. Sacred ash, amrit (honey), kumkum, sandal paste, fragrances, flowers and even letters are reported as materializing from his pictures all around the world. In addition, the followers, and even many non-followers, have testified about many miracles and cures performed by him.

Baba preaches a foundation of five basic values: Truth (Sathya), Right Conduct (Dharma), Peace (Shanti), Love (Prema) and Non-violence (Ahimsa). Although his teachings are rooted in the Hindu faith, he teaches the unity of all major world religions and says that they all lead to God. He points to the immanence of God, the realisation of which will enable devotees to become better members of their own traditions.

However, the mainstream religions themselves have not always felt that the two spiritual commitments are compatible. For example, Mario Mazzoleni, a Catholic priest who wrote a book that accepted Sai Baba as a living Christ, was excommunicated in 1992.

Remarkable as these stories about Sai Baba are, they are unlikely to convince traditional scientists until he is tested by researchers under laboratory conditions. Sai Baba considers that this is unnecessary. "Miracles are my visiting cards" he says and, on another occasion, "My greatest miracle is Love"

His spiritual teachings and the character transformation it triggers are far more important than the tantalising Psycho Kinetic (PK) phenomena he displays: 'For what purpose were you born? Man has been sent into the world to realise the truth that he is not man, but God. The wave dances with the wind, basks in the sun, frisks in the rain, imagining it is playing on the breast of the sea; it does not know that it is the sea itself. Until it realises the truth, it will be tossed up and down; when it knows it, it can lie calm and collected, at peace with itself.'

If we embrace the spiritual principle of unconditional love, says Sai Baba, we too can become a godlike being and will manifest the same incredible PK phenomena. This, he suggests, is the next evolutionary step of mankind.

So that's the story of Sai Baba, the positive side, there is another side though, that I have to mention here, and it is this, there are many, very vocal detractors of Sai Baba. They claim that he is a cheat, that his miracles are simply conjurors tricks.

The fact that he has levitated in front of hundreds of people or can materialise jewellery from thin air is explained by sceptics as simple trickery and sleight of hand. But when you read the thousands of testimonials or meet intelligent people whose lives have been completely transformed after an encounter with Sai Baba, you soon realise that to trick people on this scale would be impossible.

For example Sai Baba will often ask people "What do you want" and many people will ask him to materialise very obscure things: fruits out of season, a perpetual motion watch, a map of the world in the future, some wood from the original cross of Jesus and specific medicines. And Baba makes them appear – to keep all this up the sleeves of his robe would be an impossibility.

Even worse claims have been laid at his door, scandalous claims of child abuse from ex disciples, claiming terrible things. These claims are often challenged and many have been proven in court to be false. None the less they exist and it is true that people who were once loving disciples have become the greatest champions of those trying to promote his downfall...Sri Sathya Sai Baba died 24 April 2011.

Pete's account of Sri Sathya Sai Baba strikes right at the heart of this miracle of Avatars and yet all the known Avatars have their detractors and sceptics. Lord Krishna was faced with much opposition, Jesus was brutally and mercilessly crucified and both Shirdi and Sai Baba were faced with a deluge of hostility. There is one thing in common with the condemnation of all Avatars, human ego and ignorance.

The following and current Avatar to mention here, Mother Meera, has also faced scorn from a former devotee.

First he published a book full of love and praise for Mother Meera, however when a personal request was denied he turned on her and published another book

claiming Mother Meera to be false, a statement he some time later apparently retracted – oh how the ego is so very fragile.

Mother Meera

'The whole purpose of my work is in the calling down of the Paramatman Light and in helping people. For this I came – to open your hearts to the Light.'

Mother Meera, in the first instance Kamala Reddy, was born to Antamma and Veera Reddy on December 26th 1960 in Chandepalle, a small South Indian village. Right from birth Mother Meera knew that she was an Avatar and had come with a Divine purpose to help the planet, not just humanity but every life form upon the Earth. Her uncle Bulgur Menkat Reddy was soon to be brought into the equation. Mr Reddy had a vision/inner revelation that the Divine Mother had been born in India and so made it his mission to find her.

For many years Mr Reddy wandered throughout India in a vain attempt to locate the female Avatar. However, Mr Reddy was soon to encounter a Divine irony, for on his return to the village, devastated that he was unable to find the elusive Divine Mother, he visited his niece Kamala and instantly recognised her as the child in his vision. From that point on Mr Reddy became Mother Meera's guardian and constant attendant.

Eventually Mother Meera moved to Germany with Mr Reddy and her close companion, Adilakshmi, to fulfil the will of he who sent her, the Supreme Being, otherwise known as Paramatman. Mother's primary mission is to bring down the Paramatman Light, a power that is to transform the planet and elevate human consciousness.

Right from the beginning Mother bestowed Divine grace, known as Pranam and Darshan, not only upon her devotees, but all who come to see her and never charges a penny. This blessing is delivered in silence, which breaks away from the traditional blessings of many a guru of ancient tradition.

The objective of Pranam and Darshan is, in the first aspect of Pranam, for Mother to carefully undo knots in two energy channels that run from the feet to the head; these are described by Mother as red and white lines. The second aspect that of Darshan, is where Mother looks into the eyes, the window of the soul. In so doing Mother Meera looks into every aspect of your current incarnation and gives help with your difficulties and evolution. Mother encourages recipients of her grace to still the mind of all thought processes to gain maximum benefit, or to engage in Jappa Mantra; the repetition of Divine words/sound.

This silent grace is in total congruency with what Mother teaches, *"Visions may come and visions may go, but the silence always remains."* Answers 1.

This aspect of Pranam and Darshan will be covered in more detail by my own personal experience in due course.

Mother Meera teaches the unity of all religions, in the same manner as all other Avatars; stating that all these paths eventually lead to God and that whatever faith one follows we should become a better Hindu, Sikh, Muslim, Christian, Jew etc. The prime focus of Mother's teaching, like all Avatars, is on Bhakti, devotion to God and in that she accepts all denominations.

Mother has a profound sense of equanimity for all of humanity, at one time she was asked whether she would bestow Pranam and Darshan upon Hitler, if still alive. Mother's answer was in the affirmative, stating that we are all God's children – so, yes, she would have helped him.

Mother Meera is not looking for followers, she does state however, that whatever faith you may be, if she is asked with sincerity she will help. Mother discourages people from tearing up their roots to come and live close by to her, stating that no matter where you live, if asked her grace will be given. The free transmission of Light, Love and Grace is Mother's gift to the world.

In Answers 1 a question is asked whether Mother's work is ongoing. *'All the time. The consciousness of mankind is being prepared for great leaps and discoveries – in a gentle way wherever possible. But some things will have to be destroyed. I do not like to destroy; I like to change things. But where there is no openness there must be destruction. However, God is giving man a great chance. Many divine persons are here. We are showing man a way out; we are offering him the divine Light, the divine knowledge. We are bringing down into the consciousness of the Earth the Divine consciousness. Now man must choose. Man is free; God will not force his children to do anything. He wants their free love. Mercy and love are always there.'*

In the same manner as all other Avatars, Mother Meera is attributed many miracles. *'The Avatar comes from God and has the power and Light of God. The Avatar has a human body while God has no form and yet all forms.'* ~ Mother Meera.

31

Today Mother Meera travels each year to various countries, doing the bidding of Paramatman to reach out to ever more people in need of the Divine Light.

However, Mother does not claim to be the only Avatar currently working on earth stating that many are here now to fulfil the Divine work, some known, and some unknown.

So then, for the delirious searchers for truth the answer is out there, it has always been out there in the east, but for the western mindset – well…not quite so simple.

Coming to the end of this section on the known Avatars and especially that of Mother Meera, I decided to review that which has been written by others in the "know" about the Mother's personal path and experiences that prepared her for the Avatorial role here on Earth. Mother Meera had been taken up to various spiritual plains and not only met many Divine entities, such as the Avatars Lord Krishna, Jesus and Mother Mary; but Paramatman to.

This review was extremely humbling, so much so that I questioned myself as to who am I to write about the Divine and the path we should be treading to re-unite with our source.

As I contemplated upon this feeling of unworthiness, this came into my mind: *Does the bricklayer concern himself with the work of the electrician, or the electrician that of the plumber or stonemason? All of these are doing the will of their paymaster, it is enough to be graced with viewing the plans of the Great Architect in building the new spiritual and Divine city…*

Jesus the Christ

'Blessed are the pure in heart: for they shall see God.'

I have departed here from the chronological order of Avatars in leaving the advent of Lord Jesus until last instead of second in sequence. All proceeding Avatars have their origin in the east, Lord Jesus is the only Avatar predominant in the west.

The linear time progression of eastern and western temperament represents a Divine plan that once brought together, like hands in prayer, produce an irresistible power for the good of humanity.

Jesus was born c4 BC in Bethlehem, Judea – then part of the Roman Empire, under the rule of King Herod and is generally believed to have died in c30 AD when he was put to death by crucifixion.

Born into a Jewish family; his parents were Mary and Joseph of Nazareth. Joseph and Mary, who was with child, had to travel to Bethlehem to take part in a Roman census. On arrival they were unable to find room in any of the inns. However, they were given lodging in a manger; a word that could mean either cave or stable. It was here, in the most humble of conditions, that Jesus was born.

Within Jewish scripture Hebrew prophets had foretold the coming of the messiah. Messiah in Hebrew means anointed one and generally refers to the anointing of a king – Christ is the Greek rendition of messiah. During Jesus's life there was much messianic expectation by the Jews, which explains the reason for King Herod wanting the infant Jesus killed – there could only be one king in Judea.

By the time of Jesus's ministry, messianic expectancy was at fever pitch with numerous candidates claiming to be the expected King of Israel. This, understandably, created much unrest within the corridors of power of this Roman jurisdiction.

Ever since there have been many claiming to be the second coming of Jesus within Christianity and many more claiming to be the real Messiah out of Judaism, especially from the corridors of the Jewish Mystical Kabbalah, which eventually led to its decline in popularity.

As mentioned earlier, generally speaking, the birth of an Avatar is surrounded by miraculous phenomenon; Jesus's birth is without doubt the most mysterious.

First of all, Mary, the mother of Jesus, was visited by the angel Gabriel who told her, despite Mary being a virgin that she was with child. The angel told Mary that the child would be named Jesus and that he would also be known as Emanuel – meaning "God is with us"; this is the precise definition for an Avatar. Mary became known within Christianity as the Mother of God.

Next up are the shepherds tending their flock in a field close by to the manger. They were visited by an angel who told them the good news of Jesus's birth – from thence they departed to pay homage to the new born messiah.

Finally – there was the circumstances surrounding three wise men (in some scriptures three kings), of the east, who were led to follow a star to where Jesus was to be born. On the way the three wise men stopped off to speak to King Herod. They questioned him as to the possible whereabouts of Joseph and Mary as they wished to pay tribute to the future King of the Jews. Herod had no idea but tried to outfox them, adjuring them that once they knew would they return and tell him, so he could likewise visit and pay homage to the new-born king.

As it happens, once the three wise men had paid homage to Jesus, they were also visited by an angel, telling them not to return to Herod. Furthermore yet another angelic visit had informed Joseph and Mary to flee to Egypt. This thwarted Herod's plans to murder Jesus– in due course the danger passed when King Herod died.

Regarding the three wise men/kings, prophecy once again came in to play, for they came bearing gifts of Gold, Frankincense and Myrrh. These gifts had symbolic significance: Gold for a king as the messiah, Frankincense for priestly/holy office as pertaining to Jesus's ministry and Myrrh for death/embalming, the Lord's crucifixion.

Very little is known about Jesus's life prior to his ministry, other than he used to disappear as a youngster causing concern to his parents. Whenever he returned his parents would ask about his whereabouts, in which he would reply that he had been in his father's house dealing with his father's affairs. It is generally accepted, as documented in the Gospels that he had wandered off to the synagogue. An alternate theory is that he would frequently venture into the desert, perhaps to a cave, where in solitude he would still his body in meditation.

This Yogic aspect gains further credence in a key aspect to what he taught, in that the Kingdom of Heaven is within. To attain this state he taught that it was important to be willing to give up attachment to the world and maintain humility and simplicity – to be like a child.

Luke 17:20. *'The kingdom of God is not coming with signs to be observed; nor will they say, "Lo, here it is!" or "There!" for behold, the kingdom of God is in the midst of you.'*

All the synoptic gospels say Jesus was baptised by John the Baptist by submergence in the waters of the River Jordan. This symbolic baptism was the beginning of his ministry.

Following his baptism (meaning initiation), Jesus spent 40 days in the desert where he was tempted by the Devil; a metaphor for the outer world of duality. However, he passed the test and refused any temptations of wealth or worldly gain. This propensity for solitude gives a degree of credence to the second theory about Jesus as a child, disappearing to go about his father's business.

Jesus's teachings were characterised by parables and short, succinct statements that used striking imagery to capture the imagination of listeners. Many of his parables where closed with, "For those who have ears to hear, let them listen." This pointed to the fact that his statements went far deeper than the surface meaning and should be contemplated upon. This in the eastern Yogic tradition is known as Dharana. His most famous teaching was the Sermon on the Mount:

Blessed are the poor in spirit: for theirs is the kingdom of heaven.

Blessed are they that mourn: for they shall be comforted.

Blessed are the meek: for they shall inherit the earth.

Blessed are they which do hunger and thirst after righteousness: for they shall be filled.

Blessed are the merciful: for they shall obtain mercy.

Blessed are the pure in heart: for they shall see God.

Blessed are the peacemakers: for they shall be called the children of God.

A key characteristic of Jesus's teachings is an emphasis on forgiveness and unconditional love. This represented a departure from the old scriptures which emphasised "an eye for an eye." Jesus taught his followers to '"Love their enemy"

35

and "turn the other cheek". The emphasis on love is totally congruent with what Lord Krishna taught as the quickest and safest path to the Divine, that of Bhakti Yoga.

Matthew 5:38-44. *'Ye have heard that it hath been said, Thou shalt love thy neighbour, and hate thine enemy. But I say unto you, Love your enemies, bless them that curse you, do good to them that hate you, and pray for them which despitefully use you, and persecute you.'*

Another major feature of the Lord Jesus's teaching is the acceptance of anyone who is willing to turn back towards God, a teaching that would, many centuries later, be echoed in Buddhism. His proclamations in this respect were courageous, as where most of his teachings – they went against the accepted and divisive teachings of the religious establishment of the time. Not only did he accept government officials such as tax collectors, he rescued a woman about to be stoned to death for adultery, 'He who is without sin, let he be the one to cast the first stone.'

Jesus was also known as a healer and miracle worker. The gospels recount many miracles where Jesus was able to heal the sick, such as: Returning sight to the blind; healing the disabled that they could walk; curing lepers and even resurrecting the dead as in the case of Lazarus. He fed the multitudes by multiplying fish and a basket of bread and the most well-known, turning water into wine. This latter miracle I suspect may have a deeper symbolic significance, in that Jesus stated that his teaching was the new wine. On a far deeper level, what this simile represented was the aspirant immersing (significance of baptism) and intoxicating themselves with the Divine.

In the last months of his life, Jesus entered Jerusalem and was greeted enthusiastically by crowds who threw palm leaves, a symbol of victory, on the ground before him as they shouted "Hosanna". Jesus then entered the main temple and created controversy by overturning the tables of the money lenders. Jesus criticised them for conducting business in a sacred temple – claiming they had turned the temple into a "den of robbers". The radical nature of Jesus's teachings, in addition to his growing following, aroused the concern of the religious authorities, who felt threatened by the message of Jesus.

Later that week Jesus celebrated the Passover meal with his twelve disciples where he foretold that he would be betrayed and turned over to the authorities by Judas, one of his own disciples. This of course came to pass in the garden of gethsemane, where Judas kissed Jesus as a sign for the Roman guards, who promptly arrested him.

In due course the Jewish elders interrogated him seeking to trip him up with weighted questions, asking whether he was the Son of God. Jesus replied 'It is as you say.' The Jewish Sanhedrin passed him to the Roman authorities with the recommendation he should be charged with blasphemy. However, Pontius Pilate would not be drawn into what he considered to be a problem for the Jewish religious authorities. Instead he levelled a secular question to Jesus asking him if he was the King of the Jews, the reply of which threw the Roman legate, 'My Kingdom is not of this world, it is a heavenly Kingdom.'

Pontius Pilate was reluctant to have him executed as he couldn't see a crime committed against the Empire. In the meantime Pilate's wife had a dream in which she felt Jesus was innocent so tried to persuade Pilate to release him. So, Pilate, hoping to appease the Jewish authorities, ordered Jesus to be flogged instead; but the Jewish Sanhedrin still wanted Jesus executed.

However, Pilate came up with a plan, for on the feast of Passover it was traditional for the Roman authorities to release one prisoner; surely they would choose and release Jesus. To the consternation of Pilate, the crowd chose not Jesus to be released but Barabbas – a convicted criminal. Pilate symbolically washed his hands saying it was not his doing but the will of the Jewish priests.

Now followed the most harrowing and most shameful, despicable and horrific crime ever committed in human history.

Jesus's flesh already torn asunder from the terrible flogging, his human body beaten and bloodied to the point of non-recognition, further humiliation was inflicted. A crown made of thorns was forcibly seated on his head, Jesus was led up to Mount Calvary (The Seat of the Skull), to be crucified. He was further beaten and chastised by soldiers and some in the crowd. Many others were weeping at the sight of Jesus being taken to his execution. He was forced to carry his heavy cross and at one stage collapsed. Finally, Jesus was nailed to the cross with an inscription above his head; INRI, which is said to be a notation for "Jesus (I) of Nazareth (N) the King (R) of the Jews (I).

He was crucified in between two thieves where one sarcastically stated, 'If you really are the Son of God then why don't you save yourself.' However, the other criminal reprimanded him and asked Jesus for forgiveness, for this Jesus replied, 'This very day you shall be with me in the Kingdom of Heaven.'

As soldiers were dividing up his clothes by casting lots, on the cross Jesus pronounced. 'Father, forgive them, for they know not what they do.' Tradition has it that Jesus died on the cross, with a Roman soldier puncturing his side with a spear to prove that he was dead. Although the likelihood was that Jesus was still alive.

This act was to speed his death, for it was usual practice for the crucified to have a leg broken to prevent them from supporting their own weight on the legs – this resulted in slow suffocation as it was impossible to breath. The Gospels relate that on the Sunday following the crucifixion, Mary Magdalene visited the tomb of Jesus to find it empty. His disciples came to realise that Jesus had risen from the dead. In the mystic traditions of Christianity, the spear that pierced Jesus's side became known as the spear of destiny and is said to have mystical powers. Another tradition has it that Joseph of Aramathea collected Jesus's blood from the wound in a cup, this cup became linked to the legend of the Holy Grail.

There are some scholars who believe Jesus survived the cross and went to India. There is a small village in India, right in the midst and surrounded by the Hindu faith, that is deeply Christian. The tradition in this village is that a holy and righteous teacher called Isa/Yesu (Jesus), came and settled in their village sometime in the first century AD.

There is a uniqueness about the advent of the Avatar Lord Jesus the Christ, for all other known Avatars have their origins in India. It is here that the western mind temperament comes to the fore in the esoteric teachings of the west. Right at the vanguard of the secret teachings is the legend of the Holy Grail.

It is a tradition that God can be approached directly by anyone through Jesus – or any Avatar for that matter, a fact emphasised by every single incarnated Avatar.

CHAPTER 2

BRINGING EAST AND WEST TOGETHER

From here I digress from the spiritual, we will start from ground zero, a western man who from boyhood had been led to believe certain traits define being a man. In days gone by, across the various continents around the world, there existed initiation rites for the adolescent to pass into manhood, or indeed womanhood. All manner of trials and tribulation, from killing a Lion to overcoming enormous physical and psychological pain, or being left on your own in a cave for a prolonged period of time, were employed to test your courage and manhood.

The problem for me and just so, so many others around the world, is that these initiations or rites of passage, as a defining moment no longer exist; not that they should. OK, here in Britain we have the defining moment of becoming an instant man or woman when the clock strikes midnight on the eve of your eighteenth birthday, formerly twenty-one; now that's meaningful.

So, this worthiness was left to my own interpretation; drawing from sources available in my immediate western big city environment.

It is interesting regarding perceptions of expectation in relation to maturity, from my perspective, being brought up on a rough council estate, it was about being tough, about fighting, about being that urban warrior; in other words, the pack mentality of the urban jungle. This subconscious attitude was an echo of the bygone age of the adolescent initiation rites of the warrior.

For others, status was about social standing or education, about the job you had, blue collar, white collar or even running your own business. Even running your own business is graded upon your success/wealth.

The pressure of achievement and success in the so-called modern world is extremely demanding and oppressive. If you can't be a king or prince, be a politician, be a successful businessman, be an academic, be a professional – doctor, nurse or tradesman. If you can't do it with your intellect, do it physically in many of the sporting disciplines etc.

The caste system of Hinduism is an imposed reality, the caste system of the west (Britain especially), of upper class, middle class, lower class, still exists today; albeit in a somewhat covert mode.

For they who struggle in any of these fields, the dark side beckons; it has nothing to do with social standing, it's just…Wonga, if you don't have the opportunities to make it being legitimate, then do it by other means; in one word – survival.

The above constitutes that of which I was faced with, conditioned by my western external environment on a daily basis, as is everyone else. A major problem with the "everyone else" part of this mosaic, is that we are all continually reinforcing so many misconceptions. All of us are watering and cultivating a garden of weeds, believing that the seeds we are nurturing to be flowers; yet on closer scrutiny these weeds are seeds of deep claustrophobic darkness. And yet this was only the tip off the iceberg.

What we are dealing with here is just one aspect of conditioning, a major part of what Pete had raised in his appraisal of my autobiography, "You seem to have become a full-blown teacher without explaining how you got there". The truth of the matter is that it has been a hard and at times tedious path, a hard fought internal battle that continues to this day.

You see, the problem is that I was not fortunate enough to have been brought up in an environment of spiritual teachers where I could just trot off as a child and speak to saints, gurus or yogis. Not in an environment to be given the opportunity to run away and live in an ashram in the Himalayas or become a recluse in a forest; no I had a different type of conditioning. In fact as the years have gone by I have contemplated whether or not I'm a spiritual freak, a freak that has been set-up by the Divine as a spiritual experiment here in the manic west…how else could I explain my situation?

Pete had read the manuscript of my autobiography. I eagerly awaited his appraisal. What I love about my friend Pete is that he will hit you with the truth as he sees it, no punches pulled.

'Jim, your book is brilliant, your story is quite amazing, but…'

I sat there waiting for the content of the "but".

'When it comes to the chapter on the Master, you write as if you are just suddenly a full-blown teacher, you have all this knowledge, but you don't explain how you got there. Not only that, it's the most important chapter in the book; you need to go deeper into your experience with the Master and Avatars. You really need to expand that chapter mate.'

Pete of course was right, however there was a major problem. Over the years Pete had kept a diary of his own journey under the ever present watchful guidance of the Master; I had not. The beauty of Pete's diary is that it contains, as a western aspirant, all of his psychological and emotional ego struggles. It is a totally unique and honest spiritual account containing all of his highs as well as the lows.

So, now I found myself trying to recall over twenty-two years of interaction and guidance from my Master; the loving guidance and teaching that has actually made me what I am today. In fact I must re-qualify that last statement of "made me what I am today" – the truth is, "Un-made" me what I am today. This is poignantly emphasised in a statement made by the Buddha, when asked what he has gained from meditation. 'Nothing, however, let me tell you what I have lost – anger, anxiety, depression, insecurity, fear of old age and death.'

The question was, where on Earth do I start with such a massively important task? This question was answered in that statement, "where on Earth", the story has to start with my current incarnation in human form upon this Earth.

Every human being has had numerous incarnations, either male or female, and every incarnation results in layers of conditioning or traits; the root cause of which is free-will and ego. These layers build up with each incarnation, just like the skins of an onion. For those who are not consciously walking a spiritual path of transformation, those onion layers continue to build. Conversely, they who are searching and trying to hone and polish their inner spiritual world are slowly peeling back these layers.

Here I digress slightly, some follow the doctrine (which I truly respect), that a human can be reincarnated as an animal or insect etc. The Master informed us differently, in as much that the human status evolves gradually, from the most basic lifeform right through the spectrum to finally reach the human form, the highest in creation. It is only through the human form that self-realisation can be attained; once achieving the human form you cannot regress.

Having a conversation with Pete one day, he commented that he finally gets this reality of once a human always human until liberation. Pete eloquently explained his epiphany, 'Jim, karma is karma, so let's say a person commits murder or a man or woman cheats on their partner, or a similar human shortcoming; if you reincarnate as an ant, a cat or dog, how can that specific karma be paid back?'

This was consistent with what the Master had said in relation to humans, all other species in creation do not have an ego or incur karma, they don't operate at the level of free will; it is only through ego and free will that karma is created.

So then, over a twenty-two plus years, through the Divine grace of the Master these onion layers have been gently peeled away; hence my statement of being unmade. The truth is, that without reference to a master or Avatar, we actually like some of these layers, so we keep what is pleasing and shun anything that causes discomfort. Yet things still continue to complicate when adhering to the teachings of a Master or Avatar, the ego is ever present, even when under "direct" guidance.

The major problem with unravelling this Gordian knot of distorted truths and misconceptions, lies in the fact that we rely on partial truths as relayed by human teachers, teachings that are overlaid by their own nuances. There are, most certainly, some exceptionally good even amazing human spiritual teachers, but these are very rare indeed.

Avatars are not human, they take on the form of a human being without ego, they are the Divine manifesting in a human form to impart infallible spiritual truths. Not only is an Avatar born without ego – they come without free-will. The two Avatars I know state categorically that they have come to the earth to do the bidding of Paramatman; a Sanskrit term meaning the Supreme Being. This truth has its counterpart in Jesus's statement, "I have not come to do my own will; but the will of He who sent me".

So, as per my present incarnation, I had thirty-six years of conditioning that had in fact sent me in the wrong direction before meeting the Master. Compounding the situation to come, regarding the Master's teaching, was nine years of striving on my own, during which time I subscribed to the magazine Yoga Today, became a Buddhist for a while and read so many books, both western and eastern, on spirituality – the genre of Mind, Body and Spirit.

In due course, I began to understand the difficulties I was facing and in fact still do, albeit to a much lesser degree than in the beginning.

The yogis' culture in India would appear to accommodate perfectly the spiritual path of contemplation and meditation; there are immensely fewer distractions that the mad monkey mind can latch on to. The path of the eastern yogi would seem to be exponentially easier than that of the spiritual aspirant in the west. However, this reality is changing rapidly; the west has now infected the east with consumerism.

In the west the mind is hampered by legions of distractions, the main distraction of which comes under the heading of "entertainment". Gatherings for family and friends; BBQs; the cinema or theatre; eating out at restaurants; visiting theme parks; music at home or at concerts. This short list of activities is only the tip of the iceberg, for we haven't even got started on home entertainment, such as TV, computers, social media and the now all consuming phenomena of mobile phones...there is no time for what really matters, the Divine.

By virtue of the manic lifestyle in the west, spirituality is side-lined as nothing more than that of a curiosity. Having said that, the east has for a long time now, been infected with this western disease; *we want the same easy and luxurious lifestyle of the west*. It is a western dis – ease, for deep down it creates a profound restlessness; we instinctively know that something is wrong. Any self-satisfaction is fleeting, only to be replaced with that feeling of a deep dark void – the spiritual baby has been thrown out with the bath water.

Before you close this book, take solace in the words of the Master, for you don't have to leave this world and become a hermit: 'These rest and recreational activities are fine, but a spiritual balance is needed. Have a nice human life, but find time for the Divine every day.'

On more than one occasion, the Master stated to both Pete and me, 'How can the Divine reveal itself to anyone who is living a life of luxury?' It was and is a statement that is repeated time and again in many a sacred scripture; selfish desires only lead us into greater darkness.

Many a time have Pete and I discussed our incredibly graced situation of being brought to the feet of a Master whom we both sincerely believed to be a hidden Avatar – an Avatar here in the west living the life of an ordinary householder, with a wife and children. The massive difference in this particular situation, is that all Avatars up to this point, are completely separate/distanced from normal human family life. Yet here we were under the guidance of a Master who held down a job, looked after his wife and children and just went about life the same as everyone else; in other words, we suspected that God had immersed himself in ordinary human activity in a very human world. Pete and I had become the closest friends of this Master.

The problem with this scenario, is that the birth of a special human spiritual teacher should be accompanied by strange phenomena at the very least. The birth should be prophesied, and the room where the child is born should suddenly fill with light. Now then, that is just for a mere special human teacher, for an Avatar, well.

At the very least it should be a virgin birth, ideally accompanied by a choir of angels, or musical instruments suddenly just playing by themselves and this is just for starters. In the case of Jesus the Christ, shepherds and three kings or wise men were instructed by an angel to follow a star which would pinpoint the place of birth. Prior to this Jesus's parents were visited by an Angel, informing them to flee the land as King Herod's henchmen were out to kill the infant Jesus. However, the Master that Pete and I became so immeasurably close to, was born under normal circumstances as governed by the laws of nature; this didn't fulfil the prerequisite requirements for the manifestation of God.

To begin with this lack of preternatural phenomena didn't make any sense and created many doubts. At the very least I would have expected thousands of devotees, but there were none as far as I was aware, other than Pete and me. Many a time I would find myself wondering, what is the point of a Master/Avatar coming to the earth and not being known? I recall one moment in conversation with the Master, where hidden silently within my chirping mind-thoughts I was having doubts; trying to fathom him out. My mind was silenced when he just suddenly said, 'Jim, don't try to figure me out, it is simply not possible for the human mind; I am working on many plains simultaneously, my work never ever stops.' My mind had been read, as was to be a regular occurrence.

Eventually things were explained to Pete and me, that he had come to show the west that anyone can walk the path of peace, anyone can strive to climb the final great path (the name given to this book by the Master), no matter where they live or whatever their circumstances are. With this statement the Master also clarified "open to all", with this comment. 'You can walk this path whether you are wealthy or poor, riches or poverty are just relative terms.'

He described this so called modern world as a continual war, ordinary life had become one metaphorical battlefield. Of course, as the Master would relate time and again, the root cause of the world's ills is the human ego.

Pete and I, as rather poor students/devotees as we thought, compared ourselves to the amazing eastern reverence and worship of "proper" devotees for the Divine,

And yet here we were brought before the Master to be taught, to actually strive for self-realisation, while dealing with the demands of everyday life here in the UK; and boy can these demands be severe.

We, and in due course a handful of others, were walking living proof that we can all walk the path to reunification with the Divine, without having to escape to an ashram. It was rather strange when the Master, during a conversation about the self-realised Shivpuri Baba, had remarked what an amazing man he was, probably the most amazing man ever to walk the earth. And yet our Master didn't agree, in fact said it wrong that the Shivpuri Baba had walked out on his wife and family in order to pursue self-realisation.

The family, he asserted, should have been his first responsibility – the Master lived this aspect, always putting his family first. This incarnation, he confessed, has been extremely difficult, for the last time he was here he had come as a teacher with no family responsibilities. This time though, was very different, he had come to live the life of an ordinary human being that had to deal with the whole gamut of human difficulties.

CHAPTER 3

THE MASTER REVEALED

It was in 1994 I was introduced to the Master by David, the founder of the martial arts school I attended, not that I knew he was a spiritual Master, it was an overwhelming and powerful experience. In due course I would discover that the Master had been guiding David for quite a considerable time.

The human form of the Master stood at 6' – 2", his skeletal structure was large with muscle and sinew fitting it well; when he walked he just seemed to glide, Mother Meera and Sai Baba also just seemed to glide or float. He dressed in the usual western casual way, in the main wearing blue jeans, a smart presentable shirt or sometimes a T-shirt and training shoes. He was never flashy or showy, but always well presented.

As I stood there chatting about meditation, a powerful circular tingling sensation manifested in the forehead between, but slightly above, my eyebrows – it had the effect of making me slightly light-headed.

Of course I was very familiar with the concept of chakras, I say concept as I had no real proof at that time that they existed; it's not as if you can pop into the corner shop or nip down to the market and ask for a box of chocolate chakras, but I had read about chakras in the Yoga Today magazine.

This experience was so powerful, the Ajna chakra was doing somersaults, so I asked him if he was an Avadhutta (an enlightened human); his reply was somewhat mysterious. He went on to explain that an Avadhutta is a human that aspires upward and finally reconnects with the Divine, but an Avatar is the incarnation of the Divine that comes downward (the name Avatar means descent), with the full consciousness of God. The Master stated he had come here for a purpose.

Once again this was massively overwhelming, the human ego/mind was sent into a whirlwind spin; many of my book learned spiritual miss-conceptions were about to be torn up.

In due course I would ask him about this sensation in my forehead, he simply said, 'It is Divine light entering the Ajna Chakra.'

At this point the Master went on to explain, 'Jim, I have been watching over you for a long time now, not just in this life but over many incarnations. I have been waiting for you. We meeting now is not just by some chance of fate; just think about all the intricacies of your life that have led you here; take just one of these out of the equation and we wouldn't have met. Now then, consider this also, the chances of an incarnated human meeting and being taught by a Master is remote. So remote it would be like being at the bottom of the deepest ocean, swimming up to the surface and popping up in the middle of a circular life buoy. If a Master does not wish to meet a person, no matter what that person does it will not happen.'

It is here I wish to try and describe the Master's apparently human qualities. He is the most humble man I have ever encountered and totally devoted to his family, his depth of love is all encompassing, like the fathomless oceans of this planet. I have never seen him angry, stern on a couple of times yes, but always in total control. This complete control extends to every single minute aspect of his life. With his wisdom, knowledge and loyalty, he is in fact the perfect role model, a perfect father figure and yet this boundless love extends further. Not only is he my personal role model and father figure and of course teacher and guide, but also the unequivocal best and loyal friend any human could be graced with. The Avatar Sri Sathya Sai Baba once said, 'Why become so attached to family and friends, who are in fact just temporal. Once they have gone will they remember you? Once you have gone will you remember them when you are reincarnated? No, they will be nothing to you and you will be nothing to them; all is forgotten. However, the Lord is with you throughout all of your incarnations; the Lord is ever with you and ever your closest friend.'

His gentleness and consideration knows no bounds, countless times have I witnessed him very carefully encourage an insect, in imminent danger, upon a piece of paper as he talks to it, saying 'Come on baby, it's not safe for you here.' Then gently, delicately, take the insect outside into the garden or some other place of refuge. A regular mantra of the Master would be centred upon his love for the planet and all it holds. Often he would lament upon the ignorance of the human race, indiscriminately killing his life forms and generally raping and pillaging mother earth. With consternation he would talk about the human irresponsibility regarding nuclear power; oft stating we are not ready for this technology as we have no idea how to neutralise it. Frequently the Master would lament that not enough is being done to protect this beautiful planet and all that it holds and many times stating that we are not recycling anywhere near enough.

Now then, this occasional stern side to him would manifest regarding the human race messing up the planet; he had already stated that he had healed the Ozone – 'I will only take so much in altering human collective karma.' Fundamentally what he said is that through human collective karma disasters will come through the agency of Mother Nature.

I have witnessed people who have no idea who he is get angry with him, for no real reason other than their egos have suddenly flared...and he apologises where no apology is required. Yet others who have met him casually, again not knowing who he is, would comment in awe that his eyes had a profound depth, like that of the infinite heavens above.

If this relating to the Master's external persona sounds and comes across as weakness, you most certainly couldn't be more mistaken. Time and time again have I observed his spiritual students in what amounts to ego pleas, attempts at covert emotional blackmail; myself included. If you are on the Final Great Path and you have asked to be guided, then that is exactly what happens.

In a nice, compassionate manner, any machinations that revolve around personal self-interest are comprehensively thwarted...but with kindness. The "Oh poor me" would be met with, 'So sorry to hear of your troubles, however it will pass, the truth is that karma is karma; but I'm watching over you.' Or, 'I'm doing everything possible within the bounds of your karma.'

Whenever one of us would get frustrated with the apparent lack of progress on the spiritual path, or more accurately, disenchanted with the absence of some awesome spiritual experience, the Master would simply say, 'Yes, I truly understand your frustration, but you are doing fantastically well, I'm just so proud of your progress. I can assure you that you are making amazing progress, but you do have free will, you can step off the path at any time you wish, the progress you have made will not be lost. However, this you must know, even when I am not physically with you, I am constantly working on you.'

This quality, this subtle aura of the Master is ever present. Now for me I know, not in an egotistical way, that I have a degree of charisma, and yet whenever out and about with the Master, it's as if I wasn't even there. No matter the occasion, the function, whether mundane or going to a temple, people, whether of important social standing or otherwise, just seem to gravitate towards him. When visiting, a white man mixing within the diverse cultures of Leicester, Hindu, Sikh, Jain, Muslim, Buddhist, Christian, Jew etc. he is "always" singled out for no apparent reason, 'Please come and have some food, no, you must, please,' refusing to take no for an answer. There were instances such as purchasing such items as incense etc. 'No, you don't pay!' Of course Pete and I would then be charged double.

In fact one day I was just having a generic spiritual conversation with a lovely Hindu gentleman, when out of the blue he remarked, 'By the way Jim, did you know that there is a very wise teacher and holy white man who is realised living in Leicester; do you happen to know him?' Of course I did know him, although he didn't actually live in Leicester, but said nothing.

This inexplicable magnetism of the Master still leaves me mystified today after more than two decades. Yet really I should know better, for whenever we talked about Avatars, such as Jesus, Mary, Shirdi Sai Baba, Sathya Sai Baba and Mother Meera, he always referred to them as his brothers or sisters.

CHAPTER 4

THE MASTER AT WORK

It didn't take too long before the master assumed the role of a correctional officer, skilfully making adjustments to my many flaws and misconceptions.

Up until meeting the Master, I had immersed myself over a nine year period in the Hermetic Kabbalah, along with the yogic traditions of the east; fundamentally cherry picking what sounded good to me. I loved the western mystic idea that I would be able to travel the astral plains in my body of light at will. I was enamoured by the thought I would be able to meet up with a spiritual guide on the upper plains – whether an angelic guide or even a totem animal guide such as a wolf, a bear an eagle etc. Aspects of the eastern yogic tradition related that through certain practices a spiritual force known as kundalini could be awakened. Kundalini is described as a coiled serpent that sleeps at the base of the spine and that once awakened will rise through six chakras (wheels), located within the human body to finally embrace the seventh chakra. This seventh chakra is located approximately six inches above the human head and is represented by the thousand petalled lotus in eastern iconography. These yogic texts stated that the end result of kundalini embracing the seventh chakra is "enlightenment". Whatever that may have meant at the time and what I erroneously believed meant escaping the mundane entanglement of this world. It just sounded so good, *stop the world I want to get off!*

The problem here, as I would soon discover, is that I was being led into a potentially very misleading fantasy world. Nothing I had read up to that point had explained that this journey is in fact all about transforming yourself (unless I purposely chose to ignore this aspect) – all about ridding yourself of erroneous attributes. This aspect of working on yourself is represented in freemasonry as the rough ashlar (stone), where all nobs and excrescencies are removed to leave a honed and polished smooth ashlar.

This working on yourself was extremely irksome for many years, I wanted experiences of Divine heavenly realms. I wanted to meet lofty spiritual entities on the upper plains such as Angels, which the Master assured me exist. I wanted spiritual powers, known as siddhi in the yogic traditions. I had already experienced a lesser siddhi power some years previous, although at the time I didn't know or appreciate what these were. Here I add that such practices such as clairvoyance, clairaudience etc. come under the umbrella of siddhi. They can be ok if directed towards the good of all without expectation of reward, but when utilised as a means for financial gain it is wrong, ego building and a trap to spiritual progression.

In my early searching's I had come across dowsing, known for its results in divining for underground water. But dowsing goes a lot further than that, you can actually get answers to questions posed inwardly. There are a number of different methods of dowsing; also known as divining, my favoured method was that of the pendulum – and I was good.

Holding the pendulum in forefinger and thumb, a necklace with a pendant ring, I would ask a question that required a yes or no answer. If the pendulum swung backward and forward it meant "yes", side to side meant "no"; a circular motion indicated "don't know".

As a past time entertainment I used to do with my building trainees, during inclement weather, was to tell my chosen subject how much money they had on them. Internally I would ask the question, *does he have more than £5,* so each time I had an answer I would go up or down the scale until arriving at a figure – in most cases I was bang on the money, when an astonished trainee would empty their pockets.

For me, I just thought it a gift (no not the trainees money) perhaps a genetic one. Many years later I would be informed by the Master it was a siddhi power, a power that really needed to be relinquished. Deus (from here-on I will refer to the Master as Deus), explained to both Pete and I, that siddhi powers will come as a consequence of your Sadhana (spiritual practice), but these are in fact traps. Siddhi will lead the aspirant off at a tangent and can actually grow the ego; thereby undermining the end goal of Moksha.

Moksha is the Sanskrit term for enlightenment, or more accurately, self-realisation; knowing exactly who and what you really are. However, there was one occasion that Deus did in fact surprise me in relation to siddhi powers,

I hadn't asked for or particularly wanted any siddhi powers, so I was somewhat taken aback when one day Deus asked me to do a particular practice. 'Jim, I would like you to do the following, as long as you are comfortable with this. Choose a cloud and just gaze at it and ask it kindly with humility to please

50

disperse.' As requested I attempted this over a couple of days when out walking my dog, but nothing happened. On the third day I actually sat down on a park bench and with great focus and intent on my chosen little cloud, kept repeating, 'Please disperse, I ask you kindly, please disperse,' over and over again – gradually the little cloud broke up and vanished. The following day, thinking this just a coincidence, I repeated the experiment, but this time on a much larger cloud. To my total amazement the same thing happened and as a counterfoil, I had chosen this cloud amongst many others which just kept their own size and formation. This experiment was practiced time and again on various clouds of shape and size until I was finally satisfied it was not due to external atmospheric factors, such as wind or sun etc. I called this practice "cloud busting", after a music track by Kate Bush. Once satisfied this practice was dropped without prompt – it had served its purpose.

When I say served its purpose, Deus had previously stated to both Pete and I, if you didn't exist, nothing would exist, the stars, the sun, this world is all you. So I had actually asked a part of myself to disperse.

However, this thing about siddhi powers actually became a source of amusement for me, but most certainly not for my dear friend Pete. Every now and then, when Pete got to talking about siddhi powers to the master, the master would give Pete an exercise to do in which he could develop a siddhi. One such example was to move a pencil across the table without touching it. An extremely frustrated Pete would complain that he had been trying for weeks and was getting nowhere – oh how much I would laugh, but Pete wouldn't find it funny whatsoever.

From the outside looking in, I knew the Master was just playing with Pete's ego. To emphasise this point, every now and then, either Pete or I would have a moan or grumble about life, Deus would just simply say, 'Which part of you is getting upset?' So the game being played regarding siddhi powers was just a ploy to evoke and show Pete his own ego, the element that was getting so frustrated. The apparent frail human condition is only so by virtue of the ego – the Master does not and will not cow-tow or dance with our egos.

The ego is ever present, it will never disappear altogether (unlike the clouds) as it's needed on this plane for us to function; the aim though is to minimalize it. One day I had a bit of a moan that I was struggling with the meditation I had been given, one of focusing on the breath known as Vapasna, so Deus changed my closed eye meditation to an open eyed meditation fixed on the Ajna chakra of the Avatar; Lord Krishna himself.

Here I digress slightly. Another measure of Deus's humility was when I asked him if I should turn my devotion toward him. 'Jim, this is not necessary, so please keep your focus on Lord Krishna.'

About a month later again I moaned to Deus that I was finding it very difficult; inwardly I was hoping he would change the meditation back to a closed eye practice. Well, he did change my practice, open eyed on the Avatar Mother Meera. Deus just replied, 'It's your ego that doesn't like it, that's why I gave you this practice – so please do just carry on with what I have given you; I need you to see everything as one.'

I have to admit that I went away somewhat disappointed, or rather my ego did. But, I continued as instructed, for although the urge to change back to a closed eye meditation was strong, I had recalled Deus relating a situation to me. He had once given advice to an aspirant which hadn't been taken on board, Deus commented, 'What was the point of seeking direction if not acted upon?'

The ego is a right scrapper, it will fight for its life, for its continued existence; this reality is captured in the many ancient Egyptian stories of battles between Set (oft represented as a hippopotamus), and Horus. Horus represents our higher transcendental self, whereas Set is our ego. Horus always remains fundamentally the same as a falcon headed human, whereas Set shapeshifts; hence another representation of Set is a composite creature called Typhon. In the various battles Set, when depicted as the ugly bloated hippopotamus, either grows or shrinks; this is the status of the ego (diminishing or growing), never giving in. Eventually a truce is called between the two, which is depicted in Egyptian iconography as Sam-Tui – an image of Typhon and Horus either side of a pole. Each character holds the end of a vine or rope connected to this pole which depicts the co-existence of ego and higher self on this earth plain.

CHAPTER 5

IMPARTING TRUTHS

One thing I had picked up on in my research into the western mystery tradition, was that when the student is ready a teacher will appear and that the teacher should be revered. The genuine teacher has your spiritual progress at heart, so act upon any advice given. In relation to siddhi powers formerly mentioned, I dropped the somewhat alluring practice of dowsing immediately.

Dropping this practice wasn't that difficult, for during that chat, reason was given, *what is it you really want, to play with children's toys, or discover who and what you really are?* The same edict was given with respect to the irresponsible practice within occult circles of invoking/evoking spiritual entities to the human plain; in fact Deus went as far to say, 'These people have no idea what they are doing, they are bringing all sorts of calamity upon themselves by opening a portal for entities they don't understand, many of which are malevolent. It would be far better that they waste their time with other distractions than this silly and dangerous past-time – you would not want to go to where they are going. Yes I may help them to a point, but Karma is Karma and has to be paid.'

Deus also decried the irresponsible focus of government bodies and scientists sending out messages into outer space to alien intelligences, he said that they do exist, but not all are benevolent. So then, to some aliens, humans marinated in chili source might be a delicacy?

It was at that point the journey really began, at that point the first skin of the onion was stripped – put trust in your teacher.

Regarding trust in your teacher, intelligence is here needed. History is full of megalomaniac cult leaders whose teachings and actions are extremely harmful to all concerned. If the path being espoused is anything other than that of love for the Divine, love for humanity, family, friends and our mother earth along with all of her wondrous creatures, walk away.

The statement about trust in your teacher sounds simplistic, and it is, for the true teacher challenges your personal misconceptions and conditioning. Trust in the teacher was the first of many, many challenges that messed with my head. When I say messed with my head, the actual truth is, it messed with my ego. This thing about messing with egos is precisely what Avatars do; you ask or pray for guidance and the teachings from an Avatar (such as Jesus or Krishna), incarnate or not, and it spells only one thing…"Death". This path is one of peeling every single onion layer back, every layer stripped away to leave…nothing; it is the death of the ego; of the individual self. There is no you, there is no single individual.

Deus emphatically stated, you are your father, you are your mother, your sister and brother. – All is one, all is the Divine – wrestle with that one then; what a hard truth to comprehend.

Here I wish to point out, science already has a handle on this oneness thing, it's called atomic or quantum physics.

The irony here is that science just doesn't know what to do with this truth; every structure in place is one-hundred percent geared towards duality. This oneness has just so many ramifications, fundamentally it means when we harm others, when we harm the planet we are harming our very selves. But when we love others, we are in fact loving ourselves.

At that time, desperate for the ultimate truth, both Pete and I had asked Deus to do whatever is necessary to lead us to Moksha, to pull and push us no matter what; Deus replied, 'You have asked, so for you both, this I will do no matter what.' Neither of us really appreciated what this really meant for our extremely delicate egos. It would become a very difficult thing of beauty…like a moth attracted to the flame of a candle – an irresistible attraction to the light, and yet a fatal attraction…death of the ego.

All of Deus's devotees are given a new name. This re-naming for spiritual aspirants is found world-wide and goes back to antediluvian times; it is a tool to rid the individual of their ego name.

Consider this, your name was given to you at birth, and yet you had no concept of language. Eventually you learn your mother tongue and you will think in that language and you will identify yourself as that name – this is the first trap of ego. The path of meditation and stopping the mind thoughts takes us back to the pre language consciousness of the little child that has no thought processes – everything "just is".

Deus taught that the quickest way back to God was to offer everything up to the Divine, whether good or bad and that the Divine is everything. There is this spiritual truth finding its echo in the ancient St Clair family motto, "Offer all thy Works to God". Oddly enough, the St Clair motto is found in the core sacred text of Hinduism, the Bhagavad Gita; Chapter 5:10. 'Offer all thy works to God, throw of selfish bonds, and do thy work. No sin can then stain thee, even as water does not stain the leaf of the lotus.'

As it happens, prior to meeting Deus, it was the Bhagavad Gita that truly put me on the path to understanding the human condition and the psychological make up needed to break down so many erroneous conceptions; how to break the chains of self-imposed bondage. In fact the sacred text of the Bhagavad Gita was fundamental to my understanding of the true Kabbalah and just so many more holy writings around the world. Regarding Kabbalah, (expounded in *The Final Great Path – The West),* and the grace that descended upon me in understanding the hidden aspect to the Kabbalistic Tree of Life, Deus once said to me, 'We have been watching what you will do with your knowledge of Kabbalah.' Deus also stated that humanity won't be ready for the Great Pyramid and Kabbalistic teaching for another two-hundred and fifty years.

So, sorry to say, unless you are ready, it will just pass over your head, discarded like a computer game that you just can't get your head around.

This aspect of doing work, as stated in the Gita, without the thought or expectation of reward has caused me huge problems over the years; the western mind has been conditioned to expect rewards for your personal efforts. But not only that, like so many others worldwide, when times get tough and you wonder how you are going to make ends meet, the mind goes into overdrive. How can I bolster my income and with these thoughts come along all sorts of schemes in gathering the fruits of your actions; to make money.

Just to clarify this not wanting the fruits of your actions, it is important to work for your living, in fact Deus goes a step further in asserting that it is a duty. Problems only arise if you flame the fires of desire, *Oh, I would like a bigger house, two cars, oh I would really like this or that;* Deus's dictate is simple, only want what you need.

This aspect of detachment in the Great Work, as this spiritual path is known in the western esoteric tradition, was sorely tested in 2011. One would have thought that after seventeen years with a Master one would by now be totally self-realised – but I'm afraid that the ego is not that simple; it will fight to the utter end for survival. Perhaps there is here an element of naivety in expecting Moksha in a relatively short time. Especially when considering we have gathered so much conditioning over hundreds, perhaps even thousands of reincarnations.

Pete and I had embarked on an amazing adventure in 2007 to write a book about the martial artist Grand Master Bob Johnson, who had passed away in 1994. It had taken four years of intense research, tracking down nearly all of Bob's original students who had been awarded the status of Master and indeed many other long-term students who just had a wealth of information about the Grand Master's life.

Bob Johnson always referred to himself as the Fightmaster, even going as far as to sign students' licenses and diplomas as such; the book was to be called Fightmaster. However, at the eleventh hour in 2011, Bob's family objected to the publication, a publication that had every chance of becoming a best seller; well all authors believe their work a potential big hit.

Both Pete and I were concerned about the morality of going ahead with the publication; in fact Pete was more concerned than myself as I can recall very well.

When Pete suggested that we should consult Deus, I have to admit that I actually tried to dissuade him, arguing that we were not going to break any laws and that we had a right to go ahead and publish – but my friend was adamant. The reason for my resistance was that in my heart I already knew what the end result would be – in our meeting, to my deep consternation, I was proven right.

Sitting there before the Master, Pete posed his question: Publish or not publish, the answer was the latter, but with an add-on. 'You will gain far more by not publishing this book, something that you will come to understand and appreciate in years to come.' I was utterly crestfallen, for as this four year project was reaching its conclusion I had become very excited.

The issue was that I really wanted to prove myself (ego), to my mother and siblings that I wasn't just an ignoramus; that I had now developed into a published author; it was a bitter pill to swallow. As it happened, by virtue of the expectations of the martial community in the east midlands, we were sanctioned to do a limited self-publication of about one-hundred and seventy-five copies – most were sold on the day of the book release.

The aftermath of such a huge disappointment is difficult to pen, and yet the irony of the situation did in due course become a source of humour to the two of us.

As we sat consulting the oracle, Pete had already sat in resignation as to the obvious outcome, Infuriated that Pete hadn't gone along with my unwise body swerve, I had initiated a rear-guard action, defending our right to publish, but eventually accepting the wise council of Deus.

Yet another test came some twelve months later, when a certain martial arts master published his own limited publication about Bob Johnson, but he had stolen huge swathes of our own book without permission. What had taken us four years of incredibly hard graft, had taken only one year to reassemble and publish by this highwayman. Again Pete and I, armed with a copy of this book, sought council from the Master. Deus sat there admiring and caressing the book, telling us how beautiful it is; his advice was to sit back and do nothing. As the minutes ticked by in our meeting, Pete was becoming more and more frustrated, even angry, until eventually starting to exhibit that anger and present hypothetical scenarios in an attempt to trip the Master up; I intervened and presented a door of opportunity for us to leave.

Pete, bless him, picked up on the potential gravity of becoming angry with Deus and we left. An hour later Pete and I were sitting down having breakfast and laughing at our very human emotions that had sprung from our rather delicate egos. The irony that Pete had picked up on, was that in the first instance it was him who was totally enraged by the theft of our work, however I was the total opposite. Then the roles had been reversed; I had become enraged, but once again the pendulum swung, for in a Nano-second being with the Master I had become detached and tranquil and Pete had become angry again.

Oh, how we both laughed at how Deus had laid bare our delicate egos; a mirror that is still presented as and when the need occurs.

In fact, there was another excursion that had taken place during our research. We had met one of the martial art Masters on our journey, who asked us to teach him Bob's system. We duly obliged seeing this as a great opportunity to re-enliven and secure longevity to this system. This Master was internationally renowned, so to say that Pete and I got a huge buzz from this would be a mammoth understatement. Four years later, to the day, Deus commented, 'Haven't you two done teaching them yet?' The two of us took heed of the wise council and bowed out from any further involvement. Years later I would come to understand that this situation was not helping our spiritual progression, but our egos just loved it as we had become, relatively speaking, local martial celebrities in the east midlands.

Another hidden aspect to the book situation that Pete picked up on, was the truth of karma. If we had gone ahead with the original plan of international publication, the karmic payback would have been potentially catastrophic. However, Deus knew how much our delicate egos wanted to experience the fruits of our labour, so agreed to the limited publication. After publication came the minimised karmic payback with the theft of our work. So, how did this smaller karmic payback work? Quite simply, the family of Bob were upset even with the limited publication – following that – we became upset with our work being stolen. The following is a full explanation of karma as related to us by Deus:

In its major conception, karma is the physical, mental and supramental system of neutral rebound, "cause and effect," that is inherent in existence within the bounds of time, space and causation.

Essentially what this means is that the very being which one experiences (say as a human being), is governed by an immutable preservation of energy, vibration and action.

It is comparable to the Golden Rule, but denies the ostensible arbitrariness of Fate, Destiny, Kismet, or other such Western conceptions by attributing absolute reason and determinism to the working of the cosmos.

Karma, for these reasons, naturally implies reincarnation since thoughts and deeds in past lives will affect one's current situation. Thus, humanity (through a sort of collective karma) and individuals alike are responsible for the tragedies and good "fortunes" which they experience.

The concept of an inscrutable "God" figure is not necessary with the idea of karma. It is vital to note that karma is not an instrument of a god, or a single God, but is rather the physical and spiritual "physics" of being. As gravity governs the motions of heavenly bodies and objects on the surface of the earth, karma governs the motions and happenings of life; both inanimate and animate, unconscious and conscious, in the cosmic realm.

Wanting the fruits of my labour was historical, I had been cast adrift with nowhere to live on a number of occasions but managed to secure a home. The last occasion found me homeless and living in a vacant factory with my pet German Shepherd dog. A deep psychological and emotional scar is ever present; frightened of becoming homeless again.

I dearly wanted our book, or any book for that matter, to succeed so I would be able to buy my own home outright; the problem of wanting the fruits of your work had resurfaced.

CHAPTER 6

DIVINE GRACE

With respect to my current home, which Deus had named "The Golden Oasis". During that crisis I had consulted a very dear friend who worked in the property business, it was he who put me on to the interest only scheme. Armed with a large bundle of brochures from estate agents, I first consulted my immediate family. This pile was eventually reduced to about twenty. The next step was to consult Deus, without any form of hesitation or discussion he went through the brochures. In the space of about five minutes Deus selected one that hadn't really jumped out at me – 'This one is for you Jim.' With a background of the building trade I had my eye on a semi-detached house in a fairly auspicious part of the city. It needed work on it, but I had the skills, ego told me my family and friends would acknowledge my rise. The property selected by Deus was a very humble town house.

Well ok, the Master has spoken, so the following day I contacted the estate agent and met the rep at 12.00 pm that same day, but there was a slight problem, it was a dual viewing. The other couple, man and wife, were viewing first, so I just hung around in the background, phone calls were made as the couple tried to barter a lower price. Eventually they left with no solid answer. On my own now, the agent took me around, but there was no need. My initial indifference was blown out of the water; I just loved the house and offered the full price; it was accepted.

From here there were some pretty spooky situations that arose. Pete loves his camera and would turn up every now and again at the martial arts school armed with his camera. Nigh on always, the photos produced would exhibit "blue orbs", dozens of them. When I showed Pete the brochure of my home to be, he suddenly exclaimed, 'Look at that Jim!' There on the picture above the roof of the house was a "blue orb".

Yet, regarding my new home, things were to get even more bizarre, when meeting up with the former occupant's daughter, her mum had passed away in the house. We got chatting. I had related to her how I'm a martial artist and just love Bruce Lee and that I do White Tiger Kung Fu along with Zenyogkido (The Way of the Mind Body and Spirit), and that my favourite animal is the majestic Tiger.

Brenda's mum's name was Mrs. Lee, Her favourite actor was the martial art phenomena Bruce Lee and favourite animal the Tiger. Not only that, Brenda loved dogs and owned a German Shepherd as did I; outside of her home she actually had a statue of a German Shepherd dog.

As if this wasn't enough, as we strolled through the empty house, we happened upon hair grips on the carpet and sewing needles on windowsills. For Brenda this was extremely strange, the house had been cleaned from top to bottom on a weekly basis from early spring that year to August, the time of my viewing. There was no way that these items could have been overseen; both hair grips and needles are part of the clothes making craft...her mother was a keen dress maker.

OK, it may have been that these accessories could have been overlooked by a mourning daughter. However, for months' later mysterious dress making accessories kept manifesting. Deus was spot on with his advice, which thankfully I followed. Not long after moving in, I had a plaque made up, which I displayed in my lounge, "Welcome to the Golden Oasis", I love my home.

Not long after moving into the Golden Oasis, a dear friend and fellow martial artist moved in to lodge; Richard is also a follower of Deus. One morning after I came out of my meditation room; Richard came out of his bedroom with a look of bemused excitement, excitedly he queried, 'Jim, did you hear that?' With a rather blank look I said I had no idea what he was talking about, I had just come out of my morning meditation. Fundamentally Richard had been woken up by the sound of a beautiful melodic flute; he had laid in bed wide awake and listened to this enchanting melody. Some months previous, his twin brother, David, had been graced with a vision during meditation, the Lord Krishna riding swiftly on a cloud towards him.

Richard moved out twelve months later to head into the next stage of his life, once again I was alone with my thoughts and contemplations; as I am to this day. Some months after Richard had moved out, I awoke at sunrise and went through my usual regime. This consisted of usual bathroom ablutions, followed by meditation in my shrine room. Placing and lighting a new tea candle in front of Krishna in the shrine room etc. I went into my meditation. Something like an hour later I came out of the meditation and extinguished the very small tea candle

– I was always careful in making sure the candle was properly extinguished for obvious fire risks.

Eight hours later I returned from work, and after a cup of tea went upstairs to meditate. Entering the shrine room, I was hit by a state of shock – there in front of the image of the Lord Krishna my little tea candle...alight with a dancing flame.

At first incredulous at this spectacle my rational mind came into play – *you idiot Jim, you didn't extinguish the candle properly before going to work*. However, looking at the tiny tea candle I noted that it wasn't at the end of its life, in fact it was as if it had only just been lit. This candle should have burnt out after only a few hours if it had been un-extinguished – it was as if the Divine had lit it just prior to my entry into my shrine room, saying...welcome to the Golden Oasis.

Finally, in relation to the Golden Oasis, on many occasions did I mention to Deus my desire to secure my home outright by virtue of my previous and current insecurity. But behind these conversations was this hidden desire to make money from publishing that book; the truth is, to my shame, it was an attempt at emotional blackmail. Deep down I was hoping for sympathy from the Master and that once this sympathy was secured, Deus would make manifest my desire – a bit like Aladdin summoning the Genie from the magic lamp to grant three wishes, I guess. Well we all know where that one would lead, the last and third wish would be for another three wishes.

Annoyingly, for quite some time, any attempt at this emotional blackmail, not just restricted to my home, would be met with a silent indifference. I would always leave with a deep sense of disappointment that the Genie refused to manifest from that magic lamp I was frantically rubbing. Eventually the message began to percolate through from subliminal realms... "Non-attachment". All Masters or Avatars, as mentioned, are totally beyond any form of manipulation. If your ego hidden agenda or open pleas for help are detrimental to the Final Great Path – they are ignored by an emphatic and deafening silence.

To put all of this into perspective, these various miracles or unexplained phenomena were spread out over a number of years. The truth is that if this all happened at once I would have gone completely mad, all of this was delivered with complete skill and knowledge, with the aim of carefully and gently opening me to a different and very real spiritual realm of reality.

The Golden Oasis became my own personal ashram, as Deus had frequently advised, have one foot in this world and one in mine, it was my retreat from the manic west – on the subject of ashrams...Back in the mid-1990s, five of us, including Deus, had been invited to meet a small group of sanyasi who had come over from India to visit the Gayatri Centre in Leicester. A sanyasi is one who has renounced the material world and lives in an ashram. It was a beautiful occasion where we sat singing Bhajans (devotional songs) and doing jappa mantra; the repetition of Divine sound.

Some days later, the Master commented to me, 'Jim, to wear the robes of a sannyasin, you don't have to go to an ashram. You can be a sannyasin without trying to escape earthly responsibility. You and anyone can renounce this material world without running away; just be in this world but not of it. Have one foot in this world and one foot in mine.' He would demonstrate this as he spoke by rocking backward and forward on his legs from foot to foot.

He continued; 'You don't need to go to the Himalayas or go to an ashram, you already know the truth; all is one.'

It wasn't as if the Master was against ashrams, in fact the opposite, but with a certain qualification. First the circumstances have to be correct, that you have no family obligations or worldly responsibilities; secondly, the time period should be no more than five years, at which point one should re-enter the world to teach.

All Avatars have the same message regarding religion, both Mother Meera and Sai Baba are documented as stating, stay in your chosen religion or spiritual path. Become a better Christian, a better Jew, a better Hindu; a better Muslim etc. No matter what faith you are, any Avatar that you feel a connection with can be asked for help.

Although Avatars are beyond religion and yet accepting of all the great faiths, we would be taught aspects that are common to all. First and foremost is love and devotion to God, to the Supreme, to the Divine. Interestingly, Deus preferred the epithet for the Supreme as the Divine...everything is the Divine.

Again, common to all faiths is prayer, Deus was and is very strong on the importance of prayer, telling both Pete and I that through prayer we are connecting directly with the Divine. Furthermore, prayer goes a long way in reducing the ego – Deus asked that we pray for world peace every day.

Deus also informed us of the importance of Jappa Mantra or just repeating the name of your God or Avatar, this he told us was another tool for continual connection with the Divine, 'Jim, Jappa Mantra is far more than just words, the mantra has a Divine vibration; it actually has the power to change molecular structures within the body. You can repeat fish, chips and mushy peas as much as you like, but it will do nothing.'

Mother Meera also emphasises the importance of Jappa Mantra, 'Repeating a mantra is very important, it helps to train the mind.' One thing I picked up on reasonably quickly from Deus, is the power of the mind for good or ill.

Deus would actually give his students a mantra, even going as far as to tell the student the meaning of the Sanskrit translation; for example, Om Namo Shivayah means *One with God/the Divine.* With regards to the Krishna mantra, Hari Krishna, Hari Krishna, Krishna Krishna, Krishna Krishna, Hari Hari, Hari Hari, Hari Rama, Hari Rama, Rama Rama, Rama Rama, Hari Hari, Hari Krishna, Hari Krishna, Krishna Krishna, Krishna Krishna, Hari Hari, Hari Hari, Deus explained that fundamentally it means he who takes away, this is the core meaning of Hari. Differing slightly from the usual western vocalisation of Hari, which is pronounced with a hard "A", Deus explained it should be pronounced with a soft "A", as in "car". The Krishna mantra presented above represents one cycle, the Rama section is always sandwiched by the two Krishna sections.

Vegetarianism can be yet another sticking point, Deus primarily is a vegetarian, and yet there were certain exceptions. Occasionally we would be invited out for a meal, if the host was unaware that Deus was a vegetarian he would accept only two types of meat, fish or chicken; I actually questioned Deus about this.

'Jim, first of all I would not insult or cause unnecessary duress upon the host or company. Secondly, as regard to levels of consciousness, the fish and the chicken are at a very much lower conscious level than most of creation. Furthermore, regarding the majority of the human race, if turning purely vegetarian was to cause illness, then vegetarianism would be wrong.

Offer all food and drink up to the Divine, by not offering food and drink up, it is effectively stolen. Also, by offering the food or drink up it becomes Prasad, that is – holy.'

This thing about levels of consciousness, the Master went on to explain further, 'The whole of creation has consciousness, even the car you drive has consciousness, although extremely limited.'

Although in the main Deus is vegetarian, only on rare occasions does he step out from that discipline, Here it should be noted, dolphins and whales are not fish in the strictest sense, they are mammals that have a high level of consciousness.

The skill of Deus never ceases to amaze me, he will only impart teachings when the student is ready. It did take quite a few years before I started to perceive this strategy. Deus would for example ask you to pray each day for world peace; then many months later ask you to pray for more spiritual light, a metaphor for Divine knowledge, wisdom and understanding. Then again months later you would be asked to give thanks to the Avatar you are following, the Divine for the light and grace in your life.

Over time extras would be added to your Sadhana. Primarily what was happening, was that Deus was allowing time for each aspect of his teaching to become ingrained, a part of your everyday life.

This brings me to yet another important aspect of the Master's humility, on more than one occasion, Deus would remark, 'Jim, true spiritual teachers or Avatars do not ask or want you to bow or prostrate yourself in front of them, this we don't ask for or need. However, if you wish to do this then that is fine.' Deus then went on to explain that such a practice is good for diminishing the human ego.

In general Deus would not indulge in metaphysics, yes he would confirm the realty of Guardian Angels, of other Divine realms or plains, but he would not go into any real detail, did not pass on instruction on how to make contact with or coalesce with other entities. Deus's primary focus was and is the here and now – to move you away from the entrapment of the world and physical form...forget other entities, go directly to God or through your chosen Avatar.

From time to time my ego would become restless, even alarmed, as I would eventually come to recognise through my own introspections. The pressure being built on the ego from the steady growth of the Sadhana, would get too much for it.

Sometimes a test would be presented, such as a request to send e-mails to various organisations or individuals; even leaving flyers with a spiritual message in prominent places. To the normal western mind this would seem so pointless it would make you inwardly go *what, really, you must be kidding!* However, never were any of these requests harmful to either myself or the recipients. Eventually I came to understand it as a test in relation to giving up free will. This free will thing is a very tricky thing to get the head around, after all it is well documented in the major faiths that we were, as humans, given free will.

Right, getting to the nitty gritty of this free will thing, how on earth can you give up free will? The first obvious answer is by becoming subordinate, for example the army, you just do as you're told. Then of course there is employment, you again just do as you're told and likewise in marriage, you better just do as you're told or else!

With respect to the army, I questioned Deus one day in relation to not killing and being conscripted into the armed forces, 'Volunteer to be a medic or stretcher barer.' What a perfect reply.

But what about letting go of free will for the Divine? It is here it becomes somewhat trickier. It is one thing becoming subordinate to an imposed regime, but one that is un-imposed? For the Divine it is all about giving up self-interest, serving others in a word; as the Avatar Sai Baba states, "Love all, serve all; serve God." It is to do without expectation of reward and as it states in the Bhagavad Gita, "Offer all they works to God".

To help in this pre-requisite as towards self-realisation, Deus guided me into charity work, a real master stroke, as always. To begin with my ego didn't appreciate this at all, I was fatally enmeshed in self-interest; in the beginning it was psychologically hard.

Sai Baba: "Hands that help are holier than hands that pray." What an amazing statement.

As I grasped the metal with the charity work, a strange sense of worthiness began to envelop me. On the subject of worthiness, here I recall a pretty scary moment with Deus. At the time I had been feeling a sense of unworthiness when comparing myself to other devotees alongside renowned saints and sages, especially of the east. This particular evening I was in Deus's company when in a flash he turned and fixed a gaze straight into my eyes. Deus's eyes had transformed from the deep, soft and usual unfathomable eternal depth of love, into fierce burning eyes, eyes that registered a terrifying power and immovable will. 'Jim, do not think for one second that you are unworthy, you can put that right out of your mind. Do you think for one minute that you would have even heard of an Avatar, let alone be brought before one (Mother Meera), if you weren't worthy?' This was the only time Deus delivered a stern rebuke; it had the effect of making me very sheepish; I felt like a scolded child.

Deus continued, 'Your current circumstances have come about through your efforts over many incarnations. You have put the work in, so with the rule of deserve don't deserve, you deserve.' Now the thing is, not at any time had I vocalised this very real feeling of unworthiness – Deus just knew the contents of my thoughts.

A very recent development in my Sadhana revolves around love. During a period of Dharana (spiritual contemplation), on saints and holy people, those special folks who are gripped in a Divine ecstasy and incredible visions, I was hit with an epiphany. There is one thing they all have in common...love of God/the Divine; in other words, Bhakti. As it is so easy to get side tracked during our daily lives, I decided to add a most fervent prayer to my daily practice, 'Dear Lord, please grow my love for you, for the Divine, for Paramatman more and more, deeper and deeper, greater and greater each day.' This decision (a decision made is a force set in motion), brought to mind something that the Avatar Mother Meera had said, 'Most of humanity don't love God.' I reflected at how very sad this is, like a mother who dearly loves her children, but that love isn't reciprocated. But it doesn't stop the mother, or father for that matter, from loving their children; this is how it is for the Divine, for God, for all Avatars. It is worth noting here, something that Deus had mentioned to Pete and me, 'Most of humanity blur the line between love and lust.'

However, once we begin to focus with love on the Divine, upon an Avatar, we immediately begin to draw, to attract "Divine grace." There is a very special quality of all Avatars; an Avatar will burn off periphery karma of the devotee. Peripheral karma consists of lesser sins; or put another way, unskilful actions. But the Avatar will not burn off major karma as this would be interfering with the key component of free will...intent.

Grace isn't just about burning off peripheral karma though, an Avatar can and will work on every aspect of your life to speed you to moksha. This Divine grace can manifest in any number of ways, both pleasant and unpleasant.

The first and most obvious example, as already recounted, was the situation of being homeless, living in a vacant factory.

Being in the eye of the storm it was extremely distressing, the relationship I had such hopes for was destroyed (Shiva as the destroyer aspect), by my partner's son who was going to move in with us on his release from prison. He had already wrecked all equilibrium and harmony which is essential for spiritual growth; the future was extremely bleak. My partner had no other choice than to re-admit her son into her home, I had no other choice than to leave. This was the first and most uncomfortable aspect of Divine grace. Circumstances presented a temporary refuge with the factory (Vishnu as preserver). Then my new home manifested (the creative Brahma aspect), which now stands as the Golden Oasis.

For most it is hard if not impossible to appreciate the Divine working in our lives through grace. Perhaps momentarily we may, in a positive moment, say something like "Thank God for that!" But generally this exclamation is only a colloquialism. But when something perceived as bad happens, a fist is raised and shook at the heavens with an angry outburst at God.

This can even happen with the most ardent of devotees. John was having a particularly hard time, not only in his everyday life but spiritually to. One day, on the back of a particularly hard day he actually went into his shrine room and trashed it. Luckily for John he had gained enough positive karma not to be hit with an instantaneous thunderbolt. On a more positive note, almost immediately remorse came in, the Master had exposed an area in ego personality that needed to be corrected – rage.

So it was hard for me to appreciate at the time when living in that factory, that indeed Divine grace was at work. It was my decision, so I thought, to move out of my partner's house.

The factory came and I was moved away from imminent disaster, the factory went and the Golden Oasis came. On each of the two fronts, hardship for three months, then joy with the new home, even being sent the perfect lodger for twelve months...were aspects of Divine grace.

I had been moved from an impossible situation in relation to my spiritual striving, to a perfect environment. The Golden Oasis, as formerly stated, was and is my own metaphorical Ashram – in the world but not of it.

The workings of Divine grace from an Avatar, such as Lord Krishna or Jesus, are incalculable, seemingly traumatic events, separation from partners, having to relocate house, forced into moving jobs etc. These are just to name a few and would seem to be, on a human level, really tough which they are; and yet for the Avatar's devotees everything always seemed to work out. Here I must qualify the difference in these circumstances between grace and karma. Striving for moksha under the guidance of a Master and/or an Avatar is one thing; a mixture of karma and grace if you will, but these situations occurring when not striving spiritually is just pure karma.

One of the most poignant situations of Divine grace revolved around Pete, the company he worked for at the time was going into receivership, the proprietor and directors of the company offered to sell the business to the employees.

Pete and his co-workers held a meeting, it sounded a very attractive deal; all went away to consider the proposition over the weekend with another decisive meeting planned for the Monday.

Pete consulted Deus with what he thought an exciting proposition, but Deus advised him to stand down as there was stuff going on behind the scenes he was unaware of.

All apart from Pete on that Monday were eager to go ahead and buy out the company, Pete felt dreadful, as he was the most respected of the team. Not only that, he had become the cornerstone, the only stabilising force within the whole set-up. He informed all involved that he didn't feel right about this proposition and therefore would not be part and parcel of any further proceedings; this didn't go down well with Pete's colleagues.

The buy-out never went ahead, and this was by virtue of Divine grace, within weeks the company totally collapsed, when unbeknown to all involved (information withheld by the board), all accounts were frozen, no credit could be obtained and the utility company cut off the electric supply...the company was already dead in the water before the proposed sinister floatation.

As things transpired, Pete moved on with his life to another company, where he spent the next eleven years. This was a case of being moved on to the next stage of his life, a comment consonant with a one-time personal predicament, that Deus had made to me when concerned over my employment, 'Jim, if it ends up that you are made redundant, I will just move you on to the next stage of your life.'

Of course, Divine grace doesn't just work on the mundane level. Deus would continually advise his students to keep banking into the positive bank of karma and avoid banking into the negative. Fundamentally what I would come to learn, understand and appreciate from Deus is that an Avatar, through Divine grace, can shift karma around. Yes negative karma in many cases has to be paid, but if you have built enough credit into the positive bank of karma, the positive can be manipulated by the Avatar and brought forward to minimise the impact of the negative...nothing less than a manipulation and rebalancing of energies.

This imperceptible level of grace is continually at work in relation to transformative processes for the ardent spiritual student, shifts in consciousness, of understanding. The best way I can find to describe this aspect is a very fine thinning of the veil of Maya, the illusion of this world.

This veil can't be rent asunder all at once though, the mind has to be prepared; without this preparation the student would go mad. One example of this is when a quantum physic, his name I can't recall, after many, many years of studying the atomic make-up of the world, was sat alone on a beach just gazing out to sea. Sitting with a silent contemplative mind, all of a sudden everything just melted before him into just one unified, dancing energy of atoms.

If this had happened at the beginning of his studies, he would have been taken away by the men in white coats, wrapped in a strait jacket.

The Master sews the seeds with a comment here, a comment there, or even an unprompted thought seemingly from out of the blue entering your mind. You find yourself going away and subconsciously doing Dharana on what was said or thought – thereby opening alternate possibilities to the seemingly entrapped human condition.

Although I could go on forever, the last example of Divine grace, brought about by positive karma is this; which in itself brings in an important aspect to the human condition; that of "gratitude". How many of us when going to the supermarket or store get frustrated by rude or ignorant customers, for whatever reason, bumped by a trolley, people blocking the aisle having a chat about how Harold stubbed his big toe on a pea? Right, consider this in relation to karma; every person shopping in these amazing places of abundance has earned the right through previous karma, it is another form of Divine grace that we are truly blessed by such places. Each and every person has in previous lifetimes given to the poor, the needy; the hungry. Now the sad thing is that these very people I refer to here are ignorant of their past and loving deeds, so will be placed in a very much less fortunate position in their next incarnation; very much like karmic snakes and ladders.

In effect, from a previous life of rising on the wings of love, they will go in retrograde motion back down the path into darkness. When encountering such aisle blockades and rudeness, instead of becoming angry and frustrated, stop for a moment and look around at all of these Divine gifts on offer. Be amazed and thank the Divine for such an incredible cornucopia; then inwardly ask that those less fortunate will gain parity. There are just so many around the world who, finding themselves in such an environment, would fall to the floor overwhelmed by such an abundant gift – believing they had actually been transported to heaven.

Gratitude then is just so very important, food on the table; roof over the head and bed to sleep in, all modern amenities, cooker; microwave. Fridge-freezer, shower, job of work which pays the bills, all so often taken for granted.

A man was taken out of the body and transported to heaven. Led by an angel into an extremely busy room populated by thousands of angels working very hard, he asked, 'What are they all doing?'

The angel replies, 'They are receiving and answering prayers for help.' The angel then led him into another room that had only a handful of angels working. The man asked, 'There's not many angels in here, what are they doing?'

The angel replied; 'Receiving thanks and gratitude from answered prayers.'

CHAPTER 7

MEDITATION

The Master: "Meditation is the key to all Avatars."

For Pete and I there was one extremely important aspect to this continued preparing of the mind; or more poignantly the subjugation of the mind. Both of us had a regular one-hour individual meditation slot with the Master. In the early days these sessions were somewhat testing, in that the windows at both ends of the room would be open – all manner of noises would make their way into the room.

Initially my mind would rattle with thoughts along the lines of, *for goodness sake, why don't you just close the windows, how can I meditate with all of these distractions?* On one occasion Pete, Jason (another devotee) and me were with the master in some woods, we three devotees decided we would sit on this felled tree trunk and meditate.

The three of us assumed our meditative posture and closed our eyes, from one end of this tree trunk came a very distinct noise of *click, click, click.* The click clicking just seemed to get louder as the mind focused on this strange noise instead of focusing on the meditation. After something like twenty minutes I came out of the meditation, not that I was in it anyway; only to see the master, with full focus and concentration, clipping his nails...we all fell about in rapturous laughter.

Yet even here the Master was giving a lesson; for a few months later Deus used the analogy of the ever-restless mind just click-clicking incessantly. Meditation is, in part, gaining control of the continuous click-clicking of the mind.

The lesson of the open windows did not go amiss – by placing full focus and concentration on the meditation eventually all distractions become as nothing.

As it happens, I was already a fairly experienced meditator, so this purposeful pronounced distraction didn't represent too much of a hurdle.

71

However, at the time of writing, I had a new addition to the meditation group, Karl brought back memories of my first faltering attempts at meditation. But here there was a difference, for me I was in a mentally happy place, my dear friend was not.

Another aspect of the expansion of consciousness through meditation, along with Divine grace of course, is compassion, seeing the suffering of others by virtue of their mind-sets, the thought; word and deed aspect that can either drive you downward into the pit of despair or lift you upward on the wings of love. A very important aspect to meditation is to gain control of the thought process.

From there an understanding arises that thoughts are things; thoughts manifest. Deus imparted this fact by explaining that a plane, a chair, a house etc. all started off as a thought. In fact we are all partaking in the act of creation, we as humans have created our own reality/unreality. Deus did in fact state on more than one occasion, 'The human race is exactly where it wishes to be, when it gets dissatisfied with what they have created, then humanity will change it, but not until.' My reaction to this at first was one of despair, but Deus soothed me, 'Jim, do not underestimate the human race, it is quite resilient and will find the answers.' In fact Deus stated that the Divine had placed all answers and solutions to human trials and trepidation, on the Earth when it was created.

Taking this to a subtler level, our emotions are governed also by the thought process; in fact, our whole quality of life is governed by our thoughts.

Karl was going through a personal psychological and emotional traumatic time, so desperate he had turned to me to teach him meditation.

Karl, in his first attempt, actually did amazingly well, for although I advised him to come out from this practice as and when he needed, five or ten minutes being ample, he actually went the duration of half an hour.

Being the first to break the meditation, in order to ease everyone else out nice and gently, my eyes were firmly fixed on Karl – his face appeared calm and tranquil.

However, once his eyes opened his facial expression changed dramatically – he had the appearance of a very frightened rabbit.

Once asked how it was he related the following, 'Oh my word, I now realise what a mammoth task I have in front of me. I am in shock as to how much is just going on in my head, between trying to concentrate on my posture and the focus of the meditation I was talking to myself. Then memories started to pop up into my mind from decades ago, things I had forgotten.'

I remarked to Karl that this is the situation for most of humanity in their everyday waking life, except they just don't notice it...that's your first major step in that you have noticed it.

This scenario is common for beginners, the task ahead can seem an impossible one, but as Karl is also a martial artist, I was able to use the analogy of a white belt observing the almost god-like status of a black belt. Fundamentally it is through perseverance and time in the saddle (regular practice), that expertise is obtained.

Thoughts are things which manifest, whether material, a chair, a jet, a home design, or negative thoughts manifesting psychologically and emotionally.

One of the most frustrating aspects to this path for me, is seeing friends and family dragged into a pit of darkness by ill-conceived thought patterns. No matter how much wise council you may offer, you can lead a horse to water but you can't make it drink, is a very common and poignant cliché, but true all the same. To tether the thought processes is not easy at all, the truth is that it's a continual struggle that I am yet too totally master, but it's definitely worth the effort.

I recall well this instruction from Deus when I was thrown down into deep darkness, 'Jim, when experiencing difficulties in your life and you notice negative thoughts entering the mind (exercising awareness), just keep repeating in your mind, *it will pass*.'

For the ego this scenario is food, it throws up the question, *hang on, I'm a devotee of the Master, so why am I going through this horrible despair, surely I should be protected from such trauma?* The answer every time is that Karma is Karma, it has to be paid.

I'm by no means perfect, and yes over the years I've been tested, and yet an early discourse by the Master surrounded the subject of giving thanks to the Divine for allowing you to pay off that aspect of Karma.

In fact there was one specific bit of advice from the Master that actually terrified me, 'Jim, ask and pray that all of your Karma be paid back in this lifetime.' Now think about this, this is not just about what you can recollect about your negative actions in this lifetime, it's about all negative actions throughout every single incarnation, incarnations you have no memory of...I did pray, but also asked for mercy.

This instruction was made all the more poignant when on one occasion I asked about meditative techniques for recalling past lives. 'Jim, those practices, although very real, will serve you no purpose whatsoever, by recalling past lives will only go to upset you when recalling the many negative actions you have taken – this is true for all humans.'

As to aligning meditation on spirituality, the Divine, regular practice hones the focus into everyday normal waking consciousness upon our source... this is precisely what Deus was doing in our one to one sessions.

Another common occurrence during the hour session with Deus, would be an interspersed commentary, 'Know beyond knowing, you are not the body, you are a being of light, never born; never dying.' Or, 'Everything is the Divine, nothing is not the Divine, you, the stool you sit on, the table and chairs, are all the Divine. The atoms that go to make up the sun are no different than the atoms that go to make up your big toe, they are just vibrating at a different rate.'

These two examples were just companions to many and varied snippets of Divine information; it was almost as if the Lord had assumed the role of a Divine hypnotist. To re-emphasise the unity of all, Deus would ask you to blow out the candle, in what he termed "Arti", left hand behind the flame and wafting the extinguished smoke over your head with the same hand. This, he said, was giving yourself a blessing and returning the flame, as Agni the God of Fire, back into yourself. With regards to the hands, the left is for receiving the right for giving. This practice becomes another tool for Divine mindfulness, in that when receiving or giving a gift the correct hand is employed.

Although inwardly in the beginning I did question this as perhaps some kind of hypnotic ploy, I did in fact let go of that initial resistance. Whenever doubt began to filter into my mind I used the grounding touchstone of, *what does or has the master gained of personal value with such strategies?* The answer in every single circumstance was absolutely nothing whatsoever. In fact Deus was very firm in his assertion that we should all work for an honest living and not seek to escape the world; we should also live by a moral code, this he did throughout all his life.

After perhaps a year of personal one to one meditation with Deus it came about that when slowly coming out of meditation (his instruction being never to rush out of meditation), I would gaze vacantly at the carpeted floor; the carpet before me would just quiver and shimmer as if all of the atoms were just engaged in a dance. It wasn't long after that this very same thinning of the veil of Maya, of illusion, became a regular occurrence, no matter where I meditated.

But it wasn't just the carpet, other apparent mundane objects also began breaking up into this myriad of dancing atoms. Similarly, as instructed by Deus, I would from time to time just gaze almost vacantly at an object, such as a light switch, when suddenly a white light would start to pulsate from around its periphery. This situation, when related to Deus, was met with an emphatic statement, 'This is exactly where I need you to be.'

An edict given by all Avatars is to see the Divine embodied in everyone, this is indeed very challenging when faced with human negativity. However, God is indeed resident within all, it's just that this Divinity is veiled by ego. What may seem as individual consciousness, is in fact just the same consciousness in all...consciousness is consciousness, as a generic statement it is one of degrees: Waking, dreaming, deep sleep or Universal/God consciousness.

CHAPTER 8

MIRACLES

"My greatest miracle is love." Sri Sathya Sai Baba

Of course, it's quite natural for those outside of my head to consider whether I'm totally mad or gullible and have been led astray, not living in "the real world". First of all I would like to point out that not only am I very grounded, but Pete, as a natural sceptic also. This leads me onto not only the mysterious, but the miraculous; that which would seem to convey the opposite of being - earthed.

Prior to a sojourn with my three friends David (Founder of Zenyogkido), Pete and Jason, to see the current known Avatar, Divine Mother Meera in Germany, I had a few inexplicable not of this world occurrences.

The first of note, which continues to happen to this day, is the manifestation of blue light. Some ten years prior to meeting Deus I had been graced with the Bhagavad Gita. The book shop I regularly frequented had been reorganised, all of the mystic stuff that I was interested in, especially Kabbalah, had been moved from the basement upstairs. Wandering around in the basement bewildered, a small Penguin Classic literally fell off the shelf in front of me; it was the Bhagavad Gita. Just before returning it to whence it had come, curious I just opened it somewhere in the middle and read a couple of verses – instantly hooked I bought it. This little book, without the usual commentaries and explanations, just struck a very deep Divine resonance within me. Unlike the very abstract mystical language of Kabbalah, the dialogue and teaching of Lord Krishna to his friend Arjuna was straight forward and easily understandable.

It wasn't long before I became a devotee of the Avatar Lord Krishna; although at the time I had no idea what an Avatar was/is.

A decade later, after meeting Deus I would be driving from one destination to another, when a deep blue light, right before my eyes as I was driving along, would splash across the sky, buildings and road, as if a giant bucket of deep blue light had been thrown before me; it would flash here and there with a glow and deep blue colour not of this world. The very first time this happened, nigh on always at night, I recall frantically checking my car mirrors for an emergency service vehicle – but alas never there. Even if there had of been, it would not have explained away this other worldly deep blue light that just flashed and splashed across the night sky.

After many occurrences of this phenomena, my mind had gone into a whirl, is this real, am I hallucinating – surely there must be an explanation for this?

Months went by, interspersed with this strange manifestation, when I decided to make my regular trip to Nottingham to see Deus, it was approaching Christmas.

I was sat at one end of a three-seater settee, Deus was sat at the other end, a space between us. In the far corner of the room was a Christmas tree; this was the only decoration in the house. We were both turned at an angle to face each other, just casually chatting about spirituality, when I felt a tickle on top of my newly shaved bald head. Instinctively I reached up with my right hand to scratch the tickle when I felt something metallic on my fingertips. The tips of my fingers instinctively closed around that something that should not be there. Pulling and extracting that which was the cause of irritation and levelling it before my eyes, I was instantaneously stunned. There between my forefinger and thumb was a perfect five pointed metallic Silver Star approximately fifteen millimetres in diameter; this was no Christmas trinket for there was no whole for an attachment. Lost for words I held it up to Deus, who just sat there with a warm smile, then he spoke, 'Every now and then I will do something like this, just to clear away any doubt as to who I am.' The five-pointed star is the symbol for Moksha.

Here this leads me on to our sojourn to see the Divine Avatar Mother Meera…which culminated with the full symbol for Moksha…a crescent moon (part realisation), horns upright, with a star above it (full realisation).

I became a student of Zenyogkido in 1993, three years later four of us from Zenyogkido, David, the founder, Jason, Peter and me (instructors), were planning a trip to go and see the Avatar, Mother Meera, at her residence in Germany. Just before recounting this incredible journey, I here need to digress.

A lifelong martial artist, I was having trouble coalescing the martial arts with spirituality; a onetime Buddhist (as was the founder of Zenyogkido), I was very familiar with a central tenet of this path, one of non-violence in thought word and deed.

My martial teacher, a founder member of the British Wheel of Yoga, had introduced me to Avatars and cleared this apparent incongruence. Fundamentally it is all about discipline and re-uniting the body with the mind in the first instance.

Zenyogkido is far more than just another martial art, having at its heart a spiritual ideal. For students who wish to delve deeper it brings in the aspect of the spirit – hence Way of the Mind, Body and Spirit. It is very much akin to the origins of the Shaolin Monks of China, Monks first warriors second. The story of the Shaolin monks goes thus. A monk called Boddhi Dharma on the silk trail from India to China came across the Shaolin monks in Honan Provence, they were so weak that they couldn't meditate for very long. He introduced the Indian martial arts to them in order to strengthen their bodies. This is very much akin to the introduction of Ha Tha yoga into the original eight limbs of yoga by Patanjali – the aim of which is to keep the body fit and healthy.

The martial way, in its pure spiritual sense, is the way of peace, violence is avoided at all cost, as David the founder of this system states, *hurt rather than maim, maim rather than kill.* David has always stated, *everyone has the right to defend their body.*

So discipline and virtue is the first step, it hones and polishes the external warrior in readiness for preparing the training of the true warrior; the real warrior is the one who combats themselves. The founder of Zenyogkido states in the syllabus, 'In the humble opinion of the founder, there is only one opponent and that is the self.' In other words, the ego. My activities at Zenyogkido would one day lead to an inexplicable miracle, which you will encounter shortly, bestowed upon me by Mother Meera.

As if the miracle of being brought into the grace and teaching of a hidden Master was not enough, Pete and I would be brought physically before Divine Mother Meera and metaphorically so, before Sri Sathya Sai Baba.

Here follows the journals written by Peter and myself after our visit to the Avatar Mother Meera in 1996.

Jim's journal

Weeks of planning took place, initially there was going to be eight of us, but gradually the numbers dwindled to just four. Leading up to the day of departure our excitement grew.

The day of reckoning arrived, April 18th 1996. In Leicester we had high winds and driving rain; Jason was very nervous about the ferry crossing as he suffered badly with sea sickness.

By the time we got to Ramsgate, the weather had calmed considerably. Once aboard we settled down for the five hour crossing to Ostend, Belgium.

The first four hours of the crossing the sea was as a mill pond, Jason was happy. Then, unexpectedly, the captain made an announcement over the ferry speakers, 'We are surrounded by a force eight gale; the last leg of our journey may get a little rough.'

An hour later we docked at Ostend, again the Captain made an announcement, 'Pleased to announce we have arrived at Ostend; I have no idea what happened to our force eight gale as we were right in the middle of it, this is very strange, I have never witnessed anything quite like this before.'

Despite a force eight gale raging around us, we were on a sea of glass throughout the whole crossing; it was suggested that we were being looked after by Divine intervention.

Once we disembarked, we drove through Belgium into Germany to arrive in Wilsenroth, Dornburg on Friday 19th at 5.00 pm. Mother Meera's residence was in Thalhiem, some five kilometres from our lodging.

We booked into the Pension (B&B) and were warmly welcomed by our hosts, the lovely Veronica Schwarzback and husband Joseph, who showed us to our respective rooms. We would spend the next two nights sharing two to a room. I drew the short straw having to share with Jason, who for the next two nights tested the building's foundations with his snoring.

The first thing we noticed in the B&B was the manifold framed pictures of Mother Meera, Jesus and the Virgin Mary. The whole building was permeated with a palpable spiritual presence.

Our host had no difficulty, as we later found out, in accommodating this unlikely Divine trio, as Veronica is a devotee of all three.

Although the four of us were very tired from the long journey; especially Jason who had done the Lion's share of driving, we were on a tight schedule.

Jason took some persuading to fulfil the last part of our pilgrimage, he was that exhausted, but after showering he felt slightly more alive.

THE FINAL GREAT PATH

The four of us made our way to the B&B car park to rendezvous with other Meera devotees lodging at the B&B. This small entourage reflected the bigger picture of a worldwide cosmopolitan following. The group we would be tailing to Thalhiem consisted of French, Dutch and German.

We arrived at Thalhiem Town Hall car park at approximately 6.15 pm; the prospect of receiving Pranam and Darshan (spiritual blessing and Divine grace), from an Avatar was now becoming reality.

The four of us stood in the car park, as others arrived and milled about; within minutes an indescribable power descended upon the four of us.

This power manifested like an overwhelming and powerful electromagnetic field in and around the head, producing a state of palpable bliss. Not only that, this spiritual ultra-field was accompanied by a tingling and buzzing in the forehead; the Ajna Chakra. The Ajna chakra is the sixth and last chakra located within the human body, otherwise known as the third eye, said to correspond with the penial gland.

As if this wasn't enough, David stood silently, arms relaxed by his side, when suddenly his body began to twist left and right on the axis of his spine. Taking the lead from David, I adopted the same relaxed standing posture. Within seconds I experienced, what can only be described as a rising spiral force, rushing through my feet and legs to power up my spine; the effect was identical to what was happening to David. From that day on I continue to experience this very same phenomena; it just manifests as and when it wants. Although it is beyond my understanding or comprehension, I was informed that all of this very real physical spiritual inundation, is Divine light entering the human form.

In due course, a very loose que was formed adjacent to a foot path at the end of the car park, consisting of approximately two-hundred people. From here we were led along the path by an aid and eventually arrived at Mother Meera's residence.

Once checked in by security, we removed our shoes and entered the main Darshan room.

Rows of chairs were placed either side of a central isle, facing a modest sized arm chair, flanked by lamp stands; the shades taking the form of lotus flowers. We settled into our seats in silence.

From my childhood Christian perspective, the whole event seemed to echo what had happened some two-thousand years ago – the followers of Jesus waiting anxiously to see the promised Saviour. There were so many people now present who had been graced in being here, to be in front of God incarnate in human form. And yet, the masses had never heard of Mother Meera, and the vast majority who had heard of her – dismissed her, just as Jesus was dismissed two thousand years ago...how sad.

The whole room is in silence awaiting the entrance of Mother, waiting expectantly to receive Pranam and Darshan. The delivery of this Divine grace and blessing varies from spiritual teacher to teacher; most often it takes the form of a spiritual oration. With Mother Meera it is unique; this blessing is given in complete silence.

An aid walked in and everyone stood, it was the sign for Mother Meera's entrance. Three seconds later Mother, small and slight in stature, dressed in a beautiful red sari, glided in as if on air to take her seat; once seated we all sat back down simultaneously.

Mother's assistants led the blessings as one by one they approached her, to prostrate themselves on a beautiful woven rug at her feet. Kneeling with bowed head before her, Mother gently held their heads in both hands to bestow the first blessing, that of Pranam. The Pranam aspect reaches into and blesses the deepest levels of the soul. In this aspect mother is also working on what she describes as the red and white lines that run up either side of the spine to undo knots; these knots inhibit spiritual progress. This, so we are told, is a very delicate operation. Once this blessing is complete, Mother releases her gentle hold of the recipient's head, a signal for the devotee to sit back on their haunches in a kneeling position. Mother then gazes into the eyes of the devotee, the windows of the soul, to bestow Darshan.

Darshan infuses grace and blessings on the devotees Sadhana (spiritual practice), in order to make conditions more favourable for the aspirants advancement along the path to self-realisation. Having said that, not everyone coming to see Mother Meera is walking a spiritual path, but Mother's grace is bestowed none-the-less, to help each and all in their difficulties.

To get the best from Pranam and Darshan, we were informed that it is best to silence the mind by meditating or going into silent Jappa Mantra and/or prayer. As this was my first time, it was easier said than done. Thoughts kept invading my mind, *I'm about to be right in front of an Avatar, to be touched by God, to be personally blessed by God...*

Hang on a minute, get this in perspective Jim – this is no ordinary Prime Minister, President, King or Queen; neither is this the Pope – it's God in human form, an Avatar.

After Mother's aids had received their blessings, a que was formed along the central isle of devotees on knees; one by one they shuffled forward as each recipient vacated the prime position after they had received Divine grace.

Without prompt, Jason rose from his seat to join the que and I followed to indicate my support for my exhausted brother.

To the left of Mother Meera is the waiting chair, it is occupied by the person who becomes second in the que, the first being the person kneeling in front of Mother. When the space is vacated by the devotee in front of Meera, the person in the waiting chair slides onto knees in front of the Avatar.

We are getting nearer and nearer. My heart is pounding and my breathing becomes erratic; many years later I would discover that this is a common phenomenon. In front of me Jason is fifth, then fourth in line. Then, just one from the waiting chair Jason stands up, bowed towards Mother Meera and walked out.

I was totally stunned, we had travelled hundreds of miles, crossed the sea, and driven hundreds of miles more, then, with only six feet to go?

Author's note: In due course I understood just how the ego plays tricks and just how powerful (on this plane), the ego is; Pete's account will give you some perspective on this.

Suddenly all went into slow motion as the waiting chair became vacant, I stood and the movie moved frame by frame for me to sit on the chair, eyes now fixed on the Divine Avatar.

As I sat there on the waiting chair, just an arm's length from Mother Meera, my mind was struck dumb as I tried to do Jappa Mantra and pray at the same time. The cogs of my mind just jammed – nothing but silence apart from the rhythmic beat of my heart pounding.

The occupant of the prime position rose and I slid off the chair and knelt in front of the Creator in human form. Mother's hands gently took hold of my head and I could feel my heart pounding in the base of my spine. A few moments later my head was released and I sat back on my haunches to gaze into Mother's eyes, a deep unfathomable and eternal Divine ocean and I became overwhelmed with Divine bliss.

In those few moments, Mother Meera had viewed the whole story of my life and soul, warts and all which, truth to tell, is frightening for the ego.

Mother closed her eyes signalling that the blessing was now complete and I rose to unsteady feet, not wanting it to be finished, and headed back to my seat.

Sitting quietly now, I gazed steadily without blinking at the majestic human form of Mother Meera. As I did so a slight white glow began to emanate from the periphery of her body, which began to intensify and pulse. Within a couple of minutes this white pulsating light had nigh-on enveloped the whole room.

For some time afterwards I contemplated on what this all meant? Eventually I understood, it doesn't mean anything really, apart from that the Divine just "is". So in fact, on an impersonal level it actually meant everything. In Biblical terms it is the statement that God gave to Moses regarding his name, *"I Am that I Am"*.

Pete's Journal

Having arrived at our boarding house with only an hour and a half to go before Darshan and so many chores to do. Unpacking; showering and the conditional washing of hair, there was no time to think. No time to consider the actual situation, so occupied with the necessary and rushing to meet the six 0' clock departure.

During the short time I did have to think, deep down, I considered this rushing a blessing and looking back I was probably right.

Even as the time of departure loomed my mind was full of other more practical concerns: Make sure we are outside in time to follow someone else to Darshan, as our navigating had proved a little too uncertain to rely on with time so short. Also, was Jason even up to accompanying us, and when we realised (after much cajoling) that he was coming, then was he up to driving again so soon?

Even the short journey of seven kilometres to Thalhiem, Mother Meera's home would provide no opportunity to think. The ever present danger of a right hand road system and a left handed driver that is in contempt of those trying to follow him, which of course we were trying to do, allowed my mind to keep itself well away from the subject of where we were really going and the full implications of what we were about to do.

It was only after we had pulled into a surprisingly empty car park in which everyone met prior to Darshan, that the opportunity to consider the situation arose.

However, just as I started to appreciate where I was, all thought took second place in my mind as I experienced the gentle brush of an Avatar's presence, or what would have been a gentle brush had I been five-hundred miles away.

Here however the sheer overwhelming power was like an unseen, unfelt, force nine wind blasting through me. There was to be fair, no impression of movement, just that magnitude of controlled, immeasurable power so close, so very close.

You may begin to appreciate this awe-struck and dazed condition that I was in, when you consider the following. Thirty-six sleepless hours on our journey, proceeded by two hundred miles of business travel for my job. This was chased down with five-hundred miles on the aforementioned continental personal survival tests called autobahns. My mind was in a pitiful state as we were led from the car park to Holy Mother Meera's house.

Once inside the house I carefully put my shoes in the pigeon hole and followed David to our seats, which were conveniently placed at the back; as otherwise I was sure other people would see my head spinning.

It was about now that my ego sat back, crossed its arms and started talking to me.

It explained how stupid I had been to try to tackle such a monumental journey without sleep, how I should be at home sleeping, not here in a hot room on a chair that although not uncomfortable, was still no sofa.

On my ego went, gathering momentum; how anyone calling themselves Holy could expect ME to sit in this un-sofa-like chair for a further three hours – after-all I had been through.

As we rose for the impending arrival of Mother Meera my ego accelerated on. The other two hundred or so devotees probably spent the two or three minutes we had to stand waiting for the Mother in simple meditation or silently saying mantra, those less spiritually inclined perhaps relished the sheer atmosphere of the room. Not so I...I spent the whole time extremely irritated, just before Mother Meera entered the room my mind suddenly spouted sarcastically, 'Yes this is just fine Mother Meera, why don't you keep me waiting even longer?'

Mother Meera's response was to arrive a few seconds later and glide into the room, regally placing herself upon the chair in which she would spend the next three unmoving, silent hours.

The dignity with which the Holy Mother Meera had entered the room and her absolutely beautiful presence, had stopped my ego in its tracks, temporarily. Then however, a suited gentleman arose from his seat and moved with a slight rush toward the waiting chair, obviously determined to be first for Darshan, my only thought was, along the lines of, 'Look at that, no decorum, just barges his way to the front, pushy sod.' It wasn't long before "I" had decided there was no way that "I" would embarrass myself by going up like that.

There followed a time of immense confusion for me, outwardly I watched many other devotees individually come to their time and step forward to receive Darshan. This time is unspecified, each person decides when the time is right for them and then simply gets up and makes their way forward with other devotees who have chosen that time as well.

Inwardly however, I received a lesson in cunning, just as I countered one mental argument by explaining how I could get up and approach Mother Meera without being pushy or embarrassing myself, then my ego appealed to the martyr in me by explaining how many others, more deserving people, could enjoy blessing if "I" was big enough to deny myself, after all I had Deus my Guru back in England, and others weren't that fortunate.

The first hour was a swirling sad confused time for me, my ego in booster mode hit me with every psychological trick to stop me from getting up and I was rooted to my seat, half with fear and anger and half with intellectual and emotional denial. During the first hour Jason had surprised us all by getting up and actually leaving (I did guess it was due to his fatigue), Jim had gone up and received Darshan and Pranam, and in truth the way he didn't meet our eyes it looked like he had either a profound experience or nothing at all. My ego opted for the latter explanation despite my subdued protestations for an open mind.

Sometime later I briefly glanced at David who sat on my left. David had so far sat silently and calmly smiling through the proceedings, and one of my main problems was what I would do when David wanted to go up. David solved this problem for me when he looked up and caught my brief glance in those eyes of his, he simply smiled warmly and gestured for me to get up. My ego kindly took over, it smiled coldly and gestured for David to go first.

The reply was, predictably, a warm smile accompanied by a short shake of the head and another generous gesture for me to go first. Then as my ego seethed, I heard the barest whisper, 'I'll be right behind you.'

The unspoken inference being, "If you go then I'll go but if you don't go, then neither will I". The strangest thing to me was how I understood the scenario so very well, this kind of emotional, or more correctly, moral blackmail seemed quite natural to me, my ego completely "au fait" with the situation offered me the sage advice that, if David does not go for Darshan, sad as it would be, then karmically speaking it would be his responsibility – not mine.

David then settled back rather annoyingly and just a little too comfortably into his smiling peaceful pose. His bearing denoted unending patience, which I had no doubt he possessed. I had however the reassurance of my ego that my choice was mine and had no influence on him whatsoever.

It was, thankfully, the beginning of the end for the ego's battle on that day. Finally, some sense returned to my thinking, and as the minutes passed by my thoughts began to run along the lines of. *Well I travelled this far it's only a few feet more, and after all, there's nothing to be frightened of.*

Eventually and for no apparent reason I slid almost sideways off my chair, in an effort to keep low, and moved forward with my back bent parallel to the floor, somewhat like a soldier trying to avoid sniper fire.

After reaching the end of the chair corridor and being able to see Mother Meera directly, I was extremely "humble" and let just about everybody else go before me into the waiting chair, until it occurred to me that all the others waiting were now "humbler" than I and would not move until I got up.

So, there I was sitting in a wooden chair, my heart pounding, trying to say mantra under my breath, but my breath had been stolen by the atmosphere and by the simple striking beauty of the thin small woman in front of me, who was gracefully giving Darshan to another devotee.

Luckily, I didn't need breath, which I demonstrated as I did not breath for the next two or three minutes. The devotee in front of me stood, performed a modest bow and withdrew. I somehow raised myself from the waiting chair, took a couple of tentative steps, performed a stiff clumsy bow and, somehow, ended up on my knees with my head resting in Mother Meera's hands.

I remember very little exactly what happened, I remember distinctly Mother's fingers playing around the top of my neck and base of my skull, very definite movements not unlike a typist.

I had deliberately tried to keep my mind empty of thought, as this is the recommended best method to get the most from Darshan, but as the experience went on for what seemed a considerable time I battled to keep it empty, until eventually Mother Meera removed her gentle hands.

Then I lifted my head up and sat back and looked deep into Mother Meera's eyes and she into mine. I can't say that I felt anything particularly profound, it was all profound, although not in a showy glitzy manner.

The two things I do remember very clearly were that as Mother Meera the "Avatar" and I peered peacefully into each other's souls, I saw her image distort slightly although I put it down to the focus of my eyes at the time, subsequent events were to prove this a lie. Secondly and more meaningfully a thought rose unbidden to the surface, *'This is going on forever, and God willing it will.'*

After David had returned to his seat, I explored my feeling of calm, peace and the strong sensations around my forehead. I started to stare at my trousers, after a few seconds I could see faint shapes forming in the black material of the fabric, and the image wavered, flickering, blending in and out.

Then another thought, clear and sarcastic, entered my mind; *great, so you get the Siddhi (special power) of rippling,* and so returned the ever-present ego.

I'm still coming to terms with what happened, both for me and to me, at Darshan with Holy Mother Meera. The closest I can get to describing it are a couple of words Marika (a Dutch girl we met), had said, 'It is everything and nothing.' For me that is it – there is no more to say.

One other thing that became clear to me is that Darshan is uniquely personal and what happened to me will not happen to another, well, not exactly as it did to me. Everybody's experience is their own, some cry, some are healed, all are altered and given food for thought.

Peace is a mat on a tiled floor in Germany, amid the hills and forest in a small town, in a normal house, in a small room; looking into the eyes of an Indian woman. If you truly believe in God, experience it – if you experience nothing else in your whole life...

I love Pete's account of that first Darshan for its truth, how his ego jumped to its own defence and survival – this is the nature of our egos, it wants to continue, it wants to live not die. The ego is full of self-importance, but next to the Divine, it is nothing.

When we left Mother Meera's home that night, we all stopped for a minute or two to take in the image of Mother's house, just to savour what we had just experienced. Standing there soaking it all up, I glanced up at the clear night sky; taking in a quick draw of breath I exclaimed to my friends, 'Look, look at that above Mother's home!' There, directly above Mother Meera's home was a crescent moon, horns uppermost, with a singular bright star located a fraction above; there wasn't another astronomic object in the clear night sky.

The significance of this is that the crescent half-moon and star, as I explained earlier, symbolises "Moksha", that is, self-realisation and liberation from the endless cycle of birth, death and rebirth.

What would be the permutations of this astronomical phenomena happening, above Mother Meera's home, on this particular "clear night", at this precise time; with the four guys observing who had travelled over to Germany from the UK and this on the back of the silver star manifesting on top of my head?

The four of us attended Pranam and Darshan on the following evening, if anything the experience was even more profound for me as we had all recovered from the previous two day's journey. I was delighted that Jason, fully recovered, received this Divine blessing from Mother.

We returned to England on the Sunday, but there is a footnote to the journey.

It was dusk and Pete and I were sitting up on deck at the rear of the ferry, just chatting about our experience. As we looked across the deck, past and through the white railings at the back of the ship, just gazing at the immense ocean stretching out behind us, something strange happened.

Pete and I spoke at the same time, 'Did you see that!' I said, Pete at the same time said, 'Are you seeing what I'm seeing?'

The white railings began to flash a brighter white, it was an effervescent white light; and then they just "completely" disappeared – then reappeared – then disappeared and reappeared. The flashing bright white railings moved in and out of existence for the next five minutes as we both sat in silence totally mesmerised.

It was as if it was a parting gift, a farewell from Mother Meera to say...your experience was real and...I AM real...Or perhaps it was Pete, displaying his new-found siddhi power as a Siddhi Ripple Master?

This wasn't going to be our first and last trip to see Mother; the four of us returned to Germany to see Mother Meera again in 1997 and 1998. Pete, his wife and David would return to Germany another couple of times to see Mother at her new and current residence.

Eventually Mother Meera decided to visit various countries to bestow her blessings upon those not able to make the journey across the sea; we in the UK are fortunate that our island has become blessed as a regular venue.

David, Peter and I, along with members of the Zenyogkido meditation group, have been regular attendees for many years. Each and every occasion I am graced with the same phenomenon of that intense Divine magnetic presence around the head and within the Ajna chakra.

Every time I have attended Pranam and Darshan, at some point, Divine Mother Meera radiates a white light. On the last occasion, at the time of writing, the whole wall to wall curtain behind mother just morphed into a rippling sea of soft white light. Then right at the end, something very different happened, as witnessed by two of my friends. Usually Mother, once everyone has been up for blessings, sits silently for several minutes, eyes closed, to give a generic blessing for all present.

However, on this occasion, mother had her eyes open; like a search light they scanned across the room from left to right and back again several times. For me I actually thought that the lighting may have been playing tricks on me, Mother's eyes appeared disproportionately large to her beauteous face; they were huge eyes that burned with a powerful luminous white light. I didn't mention this to my friends that is until two of our company related the same phenomenon to me.

Here I must add, that all of this strange phenomenon regularly occurs when just gazing at Mother's picture; light pulsing, most often white but occasionally gold and that electromagnetic field with a pulsing Ajna chakra.

Mothers face will also regularly morph into a sequence of other 3D faces, male and female with varied ethnicity; this very same thing is attested to by many, many devotees of Mother Meera. The message would seem to be that Mother is embodied within everyone and...Is everyone.

This perceived message. "I am everyone and everything" found expression in a statement made by Sri Sathya Sai Baba. On one of his journeys in India, he was being driven along a road when he spotted a man beating a dog, Baba asked the driver to stop, which he did. Exiting the car, Baba went over to this man and asked him, 'Why are you beating me?' What a wonderful lesson...all is the Divine.

It later occurred to me, that in the amazing book, Autobiography of a Yogi, by Paramahansa Yogananda, he had frequently described being in front of a saint or guru; touching their feet with deep reverence, awe and wonder. Yet Pete and I had been taught that any picture of an Avatar was far more than a picture, for the very Avatar themselves are present there in the image – a fact that I had witnessed and continue to witness to this very day. To be in the presence of an Avatar, picture or otherwise, is just so, so far beyond that of being in the presence, although special, of a human saint or guru.

As Pete mentioned in his journal, every person will have a different experience with an Avatar, some profound, some very emotional (I have witnessed just so many people after Pranam and Darshan breaking down in tears), and many who leave disappointed. This apparent disparity revolves around intent; if you go to see Mother Meera purely out of curiosity you leave disappointed, go with faith and sincerity, well – a different matter altogether. Yet here there is a paradox; no-one will reach an Avatar if it's not correct – it works on "deserve – don't deserve".

Here I relate what at first seemed a kind of interim, "deserve/don't deserve" that happened to a friend; but on closer scrutiny something far more profound.

It was Bill's first time going to see Mother Meera, so I had educated him on what to do.

All was going swimmingly well as I observed Bill receiving the first blessing of Pranam, as he knelt in front of Mother with his head being held. Mother released his head, the signal for the second blessing of Darshan where Mother looks into the eyes, but – Bill just got up and walked off the stage. Later, when I questioned him, he said that his mind was in such a whirl he forgot.

The next year Bill was there again and had promised all of us he wouldn't forget this time. There he was again receiving the first blessing, then as per the format he sat back on his haunches for Mother to look into the windows of his soul. Within three seconds Bill stood up, gave a salutation, and walked off the stage.

Later I questioned him about the shortest Darshan I had ever witnessed, his reply had everyone laughing so hard that tears were shed. 'Well Jim, I did exactly as you had told me and sat back on my haunches when Mother released my head to look into her eyes, but...Mother kept her eyes firmly closed.'

Could it have been he didn't deserve the Darshan aspect? The truth is, Mother was once asked if she would bestow Pranam and Darshan on Hitler if still alive, her emphatic reply was 'of course, we are all children of the Divine.'

So the obvious answer was that Mother had remembered what had happened the year before and made a playful sublime Divine joke. The fact that Mother had given blessings to thousands over the past year didn't come into the equation; Mother Meera remembered Bill ...all Avatars are omnipresent. Mother knows all, so it was a Divine play designed to quirk Bill's mind that the Avatar is real... something that Bill had stated, humorously after his experience.

This brings me to another mystery/miracle on one of our journeys to Germany; our car broke down. At the side of the road with the bonnet lifted, Jason, a part time mechanic, shook his head – this car is going nowhere. I honestly can't recall the exact problem that Jason had identified, but the car had suffered a mortal wound.

David suggested that we should all have faith in Mother and asked Jason to just turn the ignition; amazingly the car fired up – we travelled the rest of the journey to Mother Meera and back to England without so much as an engine cough or splutter. Jason, the man who knows, was bewildered, this just shouldn't have happened; but there was a sequel.

Two weeks later Jason got a phone call, his own mother's car had broken down. On arrival Jason opened the car bonnet, only to discover that "exactly" the same thing had happened to his mother's car, which fundamentally meant it being written off by the insurance company. A classic case of karma, or car – ma, being shifted and manipulated by an Avatar.

Returning to our journey to see Mother, we had got lost in a little German village, so we pulled up at the side of this little street, hoping to find someone who could give us directions – there wasn't a soul in sight. The four of us stepped out of the car to look around, we walked some twenty metres to a tiny side road and there, just around the corner was a singular solitary figure, perhaps the last and only survivor in the village. We approached and asked, "Spraken ze Enlish?" To our astonishment, not only did this solitary person speak fluent English, but also knew Mother Meera, along with detailed information on how to get there.

OK, perhaps for you seeing these few examples of Divine intervention just doesn't cut it, and yes, I can understand that perspective and opinion for I was also once one of the legions of sceptics, perhaps even a cynic; there is the following...

This particular preternatural occurrence doesn't just happen to me, but also to Pete and a few of the meditation group, it is to do with incense. Whenever and wherever we journey to see Divine Mother Meera for Darshan, as you enter the reception area the nostrils are greeted with a divine fragrance. This fragrance emanates from the abundance of josh sticks on sale, along with other merchandise such as pictures of Mother and books about the Avatar. This fragrance is totally unique to Mother Meera, just so different to your usual Jasmine and Sandalwood. As I use incense whenever meditating in my shrine room, I always buy a good supply of Mother's josh sticks, and every time I do so this same situation manifests.

In the early days, no matter where I was in the house, despite the fact the supply was in the meditation room, this delightful scent would manifest from nowhere. To begin with I would find myself acting like a bloodhound. I would be sniffing at all and sundry, including clothing, to check if by accident the josh sticks had come into contact with some inanimate object in my house. There was never, ever a positive ID as to the scent's origin.

The most regular occurrence of this incense phenomena was as I settled down snugly in my bed. This manifestation would last for a couple of days. However, after a few visits to see Mother, this wondrous incense manifestation would extend in time, lasting for a number of weeks, even months; in fact at times this incense would manifest months apart. Of course by then I just knew it was the Divine signatory of Mother Meera, as if mother was saying, 'To me, to me, come to me.' Many, many years previous I had encountered exactly the same phenomena; but it was long before I had even heard of the term "Avatar".

It was c1987 and I had become a Buddhist, a member of the Friends of the Western Buddhist Order, headed by the eminent Sangarakshita. I had already attended a week-long retreat at the ashram of Vajraloka, located in the hills and woods of North Wales. Pretty keen to do as the Buddha had done, as in gaining enlightenment, I booked into a solitary retreat at Vajrakuta.

Vajrakuta was located perhaps two miles away from Vajraloka, again deep in the woods and hills; it consisted of a solitary caravan – no contact with the outside world.

One warm sunny and still morning I was taking a walk along a very rough dirt track through the woods. Light from the sun danced upon the leaves of the trees as soft shafts of light pierced the canopy above; birds in their natural element sung and called to each other – I was in a completely different world to the city life I was accustomed to.

Just as I approached a wooden gate that spanned across the track, I was suddenly hit with a powerful smell of incense, I had no idea as to what the scent was, for it wasn't your usual conveyor belt incense one would buy at the local hippy shop.

The truth is it really puzzled me, this scent had no business being where it was. Suspecting that perhaps a monk or an attendee from the Ashram a couple of miles away, may be hidden in the woods close by and burning incense – I conducted an outward spiralling search. As I moved away from the gate, the incense disappeared, arriving back at the gate, the incense returned.

I would like to say that on being graced with Mother Meera's incense many years later that I recognised the smell, but the truth is that so many years separated these occurrences that I can't make that connection. What I can say though, is that the Divine works in mysterious ways. Most have heard of clairvoyance or clairaudience, but clairscentience?

For me, other than that five-pointed star phenomena, I could find a thousand and one reasons to explain away some of these apparent mystical manifestations, ultimately however, I could not argue or get my head around the following.

At Zenyogkido we were practising Judo throws and I was on the mat with a beginner. Now beginners are the most dangerous and unpredictable of partners in as much as they have no idea as to how to execute a particular technique. I was thrown without the usual expert control off the mat and fell awkwardly, smashing my right elbow onto the hard wooden floor.

This resulted in a bad injury, within minutes a bursitis had erupted on my elbow, the swelling was the size of a half tennis ball. Further complicating the matter, I had chipped a chunk of bone from my elbow, so every time, over the next couple of months, whenever I placed my elbow on the arm of my settee I got a mammoth electric shock shoot through my body from the floating piece of bone.

In due course I mentioned my problem to my martial master; his advice was somewhat less than convincing. 'Jim, when you go home tonight, look at the picture of Mother Meera you have on your bedside table, and ask for help with your injury.'

Although somewhat sceptical that is precisely what I did, the following morning I awoke and remembering my supplication to Mother, I immediately placed my left hand to the bursitis on my right elbow…it was no longer there. I then continued with my examination, not only had the bursitis mysteriously disappeared, but the offending piece of floating bone had also vanished.

Once again, in relation to the Master just knowing, this story when it happened really cooked my noodles.

I was reading through Pete's diary of his time with Deus, when I came to an entry that described this very phenomena, of pre-knowledge, of Deus just "knowing" what is going through your mind. Pete ended that entry with this apparent throw-away comment, 'Never play chess with Deus!'

Here I left his journal and went outside into the service yard of the business centre, where I worked, for some fresh air. Standing against a wall, vacantly contemplating on that throw-away comment and actually giving an outward little chuckle about not playing chess with the Master, my eyes dropped to the ground just to one side of my feet; my eyes nigh on popped out of their sockets.

I stooped and picked up the little object and held it in front of my face in astonishment, it was…a little thirty-five millimetre high chess pawn that had no rhyme or reason to be there; I even conducted a search of the immediate area to see if a box of chess pieces had been discarded, but to no avail.

This thing about Avatars is for most hard to comprehend, as no doubt it was two-thousand years ago with the advent of Jesus the Messiah. My first encounter with the Avatar Mother Meera was no different; but the actual experience bestowed an inner "knowing"… however, my ego didn't just go off on a long vacation.

Returning to Pete's journal of that epic first journey, that which is refreshingly unique within the genre of mind, body and spirit, is his total honesty, he brought in the spectre of his ego.

There isn't a person alive today, with the exception of an Avatar, who doesn't have an ego. In relation to spiritual progress, it is just a question of "how big or little is the ego". Of course, this includes me; sometimes it grows, sometimes it shrinks – this is the lesson, previously mentioned, of the battles in Egyptian mythology between the God Horus (the higher self) and Set (the ego).

Over the ensuing twenty years after that first pilgrimage, many a strange thing came to pass that would challenge my ego, the ego that surfaced after that first trip that would question what I had witnessed and experienced.

The first thing of note was the regular electromagnetic field manifestation in and around my head and the buzzing/tingling butterfly effect in the forehead.

I also regularly get, when doing standing meditation, the spiral force that powers up my spine causing a twisting on the spine's axis.

And of course, not forgetting that regular feature of the manifestation of blue light across the sky, road and buildings that, like a gentle slap across the face, seems to be saying, 'Hello, I'm still here!' It reminds me of what Deus once said to me, 'I pass by and yet you still don't see me.'

At the beginning of this elucidation on Avatars, I mentioned the miracle of Sri Sathya Sai Baba manifesting Vibhutti, not only from himself but also through other mediums such as pictures of himself. Now follows mine and others personal experiences:

Many years ago, one of my tenants at the business centre came into my office for a quick chat. It was the first time he had come into the office.

The first thing he noticed was a picture of Sai Baba and, as a devotee of Baba's turned and greeted me with the customary welcome, 'Jai Sai Ram!'

The two of us then engaged in spiritual conversation, during which he asked if I had been to see the miracle at Yogini's home; which of course I hadn't.

In due course Santo, who was brought up in the Sikh faith, arranged for David, Pete and myself to visit.

Yogini lives with her elderly mother, just the two of them, in a modest town house in the St. Mathew's estate of Leicester. My suspicious and sceptical mind was armed as the three of us arrived – I was looking for the posh car along with any other fancy and expensive material trappings that would give the game away. Of course, there was none; this after all was the St Mathews council estate, where the idea of a BBQ is a group of friends gathered around a burning car drinking Vodka.

Yogini greeted us with the traditional salutation and led us into the small lounge, adorned with modest furnishings. There on the main wall was a life-sized framed picture, without glass covering, of Sri Sathya Sai Baba. Fixed at the base of the picture, spanning its width was a narrow wooden tray.

On the wall to the right of the picture, adjacent to the door we had just walked through, was another life-sized picture of Shirdi Sai Baba, which also had an identical tray fixed at its base.

The surface of both pictures had smatterings and globules of grey ash, ranging from one to five millimetres in depth; the trays of both pictures were full of this ash/Vibhutti.

Yogini explained that this ash just manifests from the pictures and drops into the trays, which she dutifully gathers, and puts into small plastic bags for her friends and other Baba devotee visitors. Then Yogini pointed to a glass panel above the lounge door, which had a fine dusting of Vibhutti, 'Can you see anything strange about that Vibhutti?' Yogini prompted.

The three of us looked at it with a little more attention and focus; there in the centre of this thin layer of ash was a perfect image of Shirdi Sai Baba etched into the ash. The fine detail was exquisite, if a human hand had forged this image, that person would have had to have been an elite artist.

The lovely Yogini then presented us with two little bags of Vibhutti, one from the tray beneath Sri Sathya Sai Baba, the other from that of Shirdi Sai Baba. Yogini then asked us to taste the ash directly from the two independent trays.

Dipping my finger into Sathya Sai Baba's ash, rather like tasting sherbet, it had a rather bitter taste. Now that of Shirdi Sai Baba's was surprisingly different; it was sweet.

On our arrival we had presented some gifts to Yogini, some tea bags and Coffee, a bag of apples and a box of chocolates. Yogini wouldn't accept them, but told us she would place them next to the picture of Sai Baba to bless them as Prasad (Holy food), which we could take home with us; this blessing makes the food holy.

When it came to us leaving, Yogini passed the apples and the open box of chocolates back to us; the chocolates had a small smattering of Vibhutti over them.

I remember having a debate with Pete about this manifestation of Vibhutti over the chocolates; Pete said it may have been ash that just fell off the image of Baba. For me, I said it unlikely as the chocolates were placed to the left of the picture, and if the box was underneath it, then surely the tray would catch the ash?

The mind and ego is strange, we both accepted the manifestation of Vibhutti from Baba's image, and yet debated the possibility of this same phenomena happening to a box of chocolates.

Yogini and her mother are wonderful people, very devout and sincere – and they don't charge a penny.

Many years later, Pete and I arranged a visit to Yogini's for the Martial Arts and self-help guru Geoff Thompson. It was a particularly difficult time for me as my German Shepherd dog, Sai, had passed over less than one month before. This is the communication I sent to Deus:

Good morning Deus, Yogini's, well, where to start? Geoff brought his daughter Lisa along, lovely young woman, she is treading the spiritual path; although not sure which face of the mountain she is climbing. I suspect it may be the same face as her father.

Pete brought Debs along, so with Yogini we talked San-Sat [spiritual], for about an hour and a half.

Both Geoff and Lisa were blown away, particularly Geoff who bonded immediately with Shirdi Sai Baba, saying he could feel him in his heart.

Geoff kept standing up in front of Shirdi Sai Baba; both were amazed at the miracle of the Vibhutti.

About six weeks previous Vibhutti had stopped after ten years of manifesting, from both pictures. So Yogini asked Pete and me to pray for its return; it started to re-manifest two days before our visit.

Yogini let us all taste the different quality between the two, she also gave us some to take away with us. All of us brought gifts for the family and Baba.

Geoff had brought Lisa along as she had an issue that needed resolving, unsuspecting, through Yogini, it was resolved during San-Sat.

Oddly enough, I, on my arrival, had asked Baba for help in overcoming or dealing with my grief in losing Sai.

Prior to going into Yogini's home, Geoff, who was aware of my grief, said that I should let it go, become detached. Yogini, who was also aware, talked about detachment during San-Sat – the very truth is that none of this was helping me.

Somehow, we got onto the subject of my loss of Sai, when Debs suddenly exclaimed, 'You can have one of my cats.' I laughed and said, 'The only way I will get involved with animals again will be to go to a dog kennels and ask to take one for a walk for an hour – then give it back.' At the time I didn't realise the significance of that statement.

I awoke this particular morning, my birthday, with that statement playing in my head, the realization struck like a bolt out of the blue. God had passed Sai with his lead to me when he was only six weeks old, he was a gift but only on loan. I walked him for eleven and a half years, but then it was time to give him back.

Just like Sai, everything in this world is only on loan from God – of course everything is God anyway.

The thing is, although only words, detachment/non-attachment tends to come across as very cold. These words tend to portray a separation, when in fact there can't be a separation. Everything is bound by love and love is God – so all is one in love.

The knowledge that Sai has returned to his rightful owner has helped a lot, all spurned by what seemed to be a throw away comment by Debs...thank you Debs.

There was an epilogue to this Vibhutti phenomenon; in the course of time we heard of another residence that was producing copious amounts of sacred ash; Joshna, a friend of this family, arranged a visit.

The four of us, Joshna, David, Pete and me, arrived at the modest semi-detached house in Evington and were welcomed by mother and eleven years old daughter. Stepping into the entrance hall we kicked our training shoes off, placing them neatly to one side of the door against the wall.

Pete and I then presented the daughter, who through love of Baba was the centre of this preternatural activity, with two sealed envelopes, David gave her a glass framed picture of Mother Meera. We had been told that if you wrote a message and sealed it into an envelope, it would be placed on the shrine and an answer would be given; likewise, we could bring something personal to be blessed. The shrine had been formed under the stairs by knocking out the cupboard – so was quite simple and open; the envelopes and picture were placed in front of a picture of Baba.

From there we were given a guided tour of the house by mother and daughter, it was astonishing.

Every room we went into throughout the house, Vibhutti was manifesting everywhere, out of walls; from chairs; from doors; even on bedding. But there was something else, even more unusual...sacred oil. This sacred oil was manifesting from the top of the dining table in a multitude of colours – it was incredible.

When we came to leave, we were handed back the items from the shrine, my envelope just had one word written on it; and not by a human hand I might add... "YES!" The meaning of which will forever remain personal – but I can say it was profound.

But the biggest wow was yet to come, David's picture of Mother Meera had sacred ash behind the glass, but not just the usual/unusual grey ash, there was a multitude of colours, blue, yellow, red, orange etc. Dispelling any thought of contrivance here, is the fact that the back of the framed picture was taped with traditional picture framing tape that was impossible to remove without knowing it had been disturbed.

Amazed we ambled over to the door to put our shoes back on, all three pairs were covered in grey Vibhutti.

Some six months later a friend expressed an interest in visiting this miraculous house, so I made some enquiries. Sadly, the couple had stopped the visits as there were so many people coming to their home it was interfering with their daughter's studies. Again, the veracity of what was happening here can be measured by the fact no charges were made, in fact the situation had finally caused the family a great deal of inconvenience.

Returning briefly to the passing away of Sai, shortly after my epiphany regarding handing Sai back to God, I was graced with an incredible Divine presence.

For some time after Sai passed strange things were happening in the house. The first week I would be woken up in the night to hear Sai whimpering at the foot of the stairs. The last couple of years of his life he couldn't make it up the stairs because of his arthritic hips. To begin with I thought that my grief was causing me to hear things. One night awaking to his cries I sat bolt upright in bed, stilling the mind for a few moments and just listened – his whimper returned.

I know this will come across as incredulous, but I speak the truth, I called out to him, 'Come-on then!' But all went silent, so I laid back down on my side. My double bed was tucked into one corner of the room with one wall running the length of the bed. As I lay still I was sure I heard a sound of *thud ump – thud ump – thud ump;* Sai climbing the stairs – then silence. The thought flashed through my mind, *get a grip Jim, you're going mad.*

At that point I nearly jumped out of my skin as my bed jolted with the weight of my German Shepherd jumping onto the foot of the mattress – I froze.

Then I felt his movement as he made his way up the bed to snuggle against me back to back, my thoughts were along the lines of, *is this really happening?* The truth suddenly manifested when I was shunted about a foot across the bed, it was as if Sai had placed his four giant paws against the wall and shoved me along to make room.

During this time, I would, over the next six weeks, make my way down stairs in the morning to find his paw prints etched into the carpet in front of the TV and adjacent the radiator where he used to sleep.

It was about this time that Deus said to me, 'Jim, I have been looking after Sai for you, as soon as you're ready let me know when it's ok to take him to where he should now be.' With that I affirmed it would be ok to let him go. Initially it was hard when Sai's presence disappeared – however...

One night, shortly after the visit to Yogini's with Geoff and co, I was sitting watching TV, I can't recall exactly what it was I was watching, but my attention was soon diverted to watching something of far greater importance. It seemed to manifest from behind the curtain adjacent and slightly behind my TV – a blue light not of this world, not to dissimilar from the blue splashes of light I frequently witnessed whilst driving.

This blue sheet of light crept from behind the curtain and then formulated a blue orb behind, but slightly above my TV. It was about thirty inches in diameter, pulsing and swirling as it bobbed up and down as if dancing. This incredible Divine presence held me spellbound for what seemed an age; on reflection it lasted the best part of three minutes before dematerialising...I was finally able to let go of my loss.

This omnipresence brings me to another important subject, dreams. There is the relatively popular genre of dream interpretation, with many books going into great detail of symbolic meaning. Deus shed some light on this: 'Generally speaking Jim, dreams are meaningless. Dreams are fundamentally a release valve for the subconscious of all the clutter that filters its way into the subconscious mind. However, it is a very different matter with Avatar dreams, if you are graced with an Avatar dream they are real and should be taken seriously.'

I have been graced over the years with a number of Avatar dreams; these however remain personal to me, with these two exceptions.

As I mentioned, after reading the Bhagavad Gita I had become a Krishna devotee, one night I had a very profound dream. I was walking through a wooded area with a close friend, I couldn't identify my friend as there was no physical appearance – it was a case of a strong sense of presence. The two of us came across a giant tree, which was revealed to me as the "Krishna Tree". I stood there looking up at its vastness and just knew instinctively I had to climb it; I said to my friend, 'I'm going to climb this, are you with me?' My friend declined, saying he was not ready to take on such an ascent, and withdrew.

I began to climb the tree which consisted of various levels, the first was that of our apparent mortality. This first level was populated by guards armed with swords which I engaged with in a ferocious battle. Although I despatched numerous guards, in the course of battle I was run through on at least three occasions, which should have been fatal...I just stood there amazed that I was still alive – I couldn't be killed.

On this realisation I dismissed any concerns about the guards and decided to ascend to the next level.

This next level was populated by seductress women, the whole scene reminded me of the ancient Greek fable of the Sirens, attempting to lure Jason and the Argonauts to their death on an island.

After entering this realm of desires, I awoke, with one prominent thought in my mind. My friend who declined the journey, was Jason, one of the company who went over to Germany to see Mother Meera. Just a few weeks later, Jason retired from Zenyogkido; I have only seen Jason a handful of times since. For me, I continue to metaphorically climb this internal Krishna Tree to this day, no matter how slow the ascent may be.

I was in an attic/upper room and perceived I was in a dream within a dream. My consciousness shifted from that of the mind/body/internal to external. This consciousness was panoramic/all encompassing – it had the quality of clear crystal or clear pure water; it is hard for words to describe. A very positive thought affirmation entered this consciousness, which was the real me, 'Ah – so this is God consciousness.' There was a feeling of great happiness. It seemed to me that Krishna was present. After a short while I re-entered what seemed to be body consciousness again, which was more like a silent awareness in my head.

Then I was prompted to push my right forefinger through the brick gable end of this upper room. As I pressed my finger against the perpendicular mortar joint, all of the bricks started to separate as all of the mortar that held them together just started falling apart.

I could see outside through these crumbling joints, it was as if my consciousness was expanding once again to that former panoramic consciousness, but this time with a difference. This consciousness was now both external and internal at the same time. Then another prompt came to me, 'Be careful, else the whole structure will collapse.' I became a bit concerned and sought out my mother, who advised me to seek out my father to repair the wall.

I understood that with this God consciousness came "Great Responsibility".

Shortly thereafter I picked up a miniature obelic that a friend had brought back from China which had been inscribed with, "The Way of the Mind, Body and Spirit" in Chinese characters. From that I understood that I had created this human form and entered into it, then another thought entered, That God consciousness was a memory, then that changed as a tiny human body, which I knew was me, that I viewed from above, was now in fact just a memory – these two perspectives seemed to interchange; until the actual word "memory" became nonsensical and meaningless.

The whole time it was as if Krishna was there, and also Pete – who was following me following that presence of Krishna over a sun kissed gentle green hilly terrain.

This was so real that when I awoke from this dream within a dream – I actually tried to push my finger through the bedroom wall behind my head.

Shortly after awaking and trying to push my finger through the wall, yet another understanding came to me. The bricks represented the building blocks of this world, a world of solid matter that in fact is just an illusion. These bricks also represented the apparent confines of the human form – this whole vision seemed like the beginning of microcosm merging with macrocosm; internal with external. I also knew that these two dreams related to the Tree of Life, which you will encounter later.

So then, what exactly does this type of phenomena mean, what is the point? Fundamentally it is a Divine calling card, a signatory that bolsters faith, that indeed the Divine is real, that there is far more to life than we as humans know and that life goes on after the death of the body – it especially encourages the aspirant to press on for self and God realisation.

Battles have been won, more are to come I'm sure, it is in fact an internal war, that through introspection, is dictated by the "silent voice of conscience". Here I need to qualify what I here refer to as conscience. As a generic statement there are two types of conscience. The generic that is governed by external teachings of morality and virtue found in, but not exclusive to, the many and varied faiths. Then there is the specific; that which comes into play when under the ever-present watchful guidance of an Avatar. With the former a multiple of excuses can be found to not listen to that irksome still small voice that says, no, this is wrong. However, when under the guidance of a Master or an Avatar, incarnate or discarnate, that still small voice is overwhelmingly powerful. You just know that the Divine is ever present there within you watching every nanosecond of your life; omniscient, omnipresent and omnipotent...it is almost impossible to be ignored. These next two examples go to demonstrate the veracity of this omnipresence.

Pete and I had met up one afternoon in a public house just around the corner from where I work for some lunch. The Charnwood, known locally as the "Charny", was one heck of a rough pub. That Pete and I were sat there casually chatting away about spirituality, just didn't fit in with our surroundings. The two of us perceived this incongruence as we took note of the clientele and then...we were both simultaneously blasted. No, not blasted by the gangsters who frequented this choice venue, it was that Divine magnetic omnipresent field swirling around and caressing our heads. As we looked across the table at each other words were not needed – we both burst out in sublime laughter; this presence was so intense and powerful you could have cut a slice off and put it into a bag. Deus was just letting us both know he is always with us.

This next incident was not quite so pleasant. For a long time I had been mentally and emotionally traumatised in my personal life. One afternoon I had decided to pay a visit to an old local pub to see some friends I hadn't seen for years. Sitting at the bar all was fine as I exchanged pleasantries with old acquaintances when, suddenly – and without reason, the room and my head began to spin.

I couldn't get my breath and my heart began to race and pump so hard, I thought it was going to explode. Internally I screamed, *'Oh my God, what's happening.'*

Then, a split second after the internal scream, my phone rang, 'Jim, are you OK?' 'No, not really,' I then went on to explain to Deus my situation, following which advice was given how to remedy the situation with a series of breathing techniques. Once applied all went back to normal.

This was and is the only time ever that Deus has actually contacted me on my mobile phone; a time for me of great duress.

It turned out that I was having a panic attack, caused by years of mental and emotional trauma being suppressed into the subconscious mind. Later in conversation with Deus, where I gave thanks for his help, his reply was profound, 'Well, I do have to look after me.'

On the back of this, Deus passed over a little note, it was dated January 2000:
Jim,
You know who I am, you know who you are. Turn as much of your love and attention as you can to the Divine.

THE FINAL GREAT PATH

Keep strong, I am with you always – LEAN ON ME. You have come this far, let us complete the journey,

All and everything is one, Paramatman, realise – push...Yours Deus.

Finally, before moving on from my personal experience with the Master, I relate this experience of one of the master's devotees. Like Pete and me, David was having personal meditations with Deus.

I saw Lord Krishna standing on a big lotus flower in the middle of a lake, which was surrounded by trees. I then saw a path on the other side of the lake and knew I had to reach the path – but how?

Then I saw a small wooden rowing boat, so I sat in it and it moved across the water to the path.

I got out of the boat and stepped onto the path. This path was pitch black – I could not see anything at all; then I saw Krishna on his lotus in front of me, showing me the way, so I followed him. At that point the wind picked up and it went very cool.

The path went on for a very long time – then I saw a light which got bigger and bigger, the next thing I knew I was standing in this brilliant white light/mist/sea.

Krishna was still with me. As I stepped into the light the wind dropped and the sun shone.

Then I started to swim and play around in the light and as I did so the wind picked up and it went very cool again. I then realised I was messing around and wasting time, so I climbed back out of the water and back onto the path and started walking – the weather then improved.

On the edge of the path I met Sai Baba and he shook my hand and welcomed me, saying, 'I knew you would make it, so glad you could join us.'

I then saw a brighter white light coming from a doorway and stood by the door. Krishna then said, 'You can go through it if you wish, but you have to know it won't be easy – it will be hard at times. You will have to learn to give and forgive and to love...' So I walked through the door and came out into a beautiful meadow surrounded by trees with a stream in the middle; the wind stopped as my face was hit by the sunshine.

I turned around to look at the doorway and thought, shall I go back? But I hesitated and decided to stay there and try to do the things asked of me. Then I saw down in the meadow and took in the beauty – there was then a quiet voice asking me to return to the body... Vision during meditation dated 30th August 1999:

Other than absolute faith in God then, to guide your footsteps, it has already been asserted that only an Avatar can lead an aspiring human all the way to the consummation of the final great path. This is what Jesus meant when he stated, 'No one comes to the Father except through me.' An Avatar does not have to be incarnate, once an Avatar always an Avatar, with or without a physical body. A human guru can only lead you part of the way, even the loftiest human teacher who has attained to self-realization and is known as an Avadhutta. An Avadhutta is a pure one who is no longer fooled by the world of Maya, the world of illusion, a human who sees all of creation as the Divine, as Sahaja, can only lead human's part of the way.

PART TWO

KILLING ME SOFTLY

CHAPTER 9

DIALOG WITH THE MASTER

Moving on then from my own personal and intimate relationship with the Master, to compliment and consolidate that which has proceeded, I have here included a devotee question and Master answer section.

The aim of this section is to help in the practical application for the quest of your personal Holy Grail – that of Moksha/Self Realisation and liberation. The instruction given is in perfect harmony with all Avatars, past, present and that which is yet to come.

What is set out here is a compilation of notes and verbal instruction given by the Master to some of his students.

The Master's students are every day ordinary people, some with families some not. Their jobs or careers vary widely; Directors, Managers, Builders, Reps, Care and Community workers to name just a few. They all have one thing in common though, a thirst for knowledge and wisdom, coupled with the urge to understand the human condition and to find their way back home to the Divine.

The ensuing guidance given from the Master to the aspirant actually represents many years of striving by the student and was never presented to a devotee enblock. The knowledge and instruction was always *drip-fed* at the pace and development of the individual. If you are embarking on the journey home please keep coming back to this little book whenever you feel the need for direction or inspiration. Don't be surprised if you pick up this book again in six months only to discover teachings you seem to have missed. Much will resonate in your first reading, much will not. As you grow your vibrational rate will change, with this that which you missed before will suddenly resonate.

It is very difficult if not impossible to portray the pure beauty of the Master's amazing, ever present, sensitivity and awareness for the devotee's situation.

Through the Master's skill the aspiring student is gently eased ever closer to the summit of the Holy Mountain.

It is my hope that the way this is presented will help all aspirants on this at times very difficult path, to meet the many challenges that all aspirants are faced with on the quest for liberation. There will be many questions, doubts, and fears etc. and although this path is at times very trying (it has to be that way by the very nature of the goal, which is communion and absorption into the Divine), it can also be a very beautiful and exciting journey.

A willingness to change, openness to transformation, is the key to steady progress, do not expect a sudden explosion of light, the "*realisation explosion*", no – such experiences are very rare indeed, for in most cases if this were to happen the aspirant would instantly become insane; the human condition just doesn't have the capacity for absorbing and understanding such power.

Unlike going to college or university where the goal of a doctorate, a degree etc. can be seen, measured, planned and attained in a number of years, this at times lonely path can't be fixed or planned for in the same way. There is however a great comfort, for when I say lonely, it's only a mental construct, the truth is that once you have grown that inner intimate connection with an Avatar, you are never ever alone.

The aspirant must always keep in mind that like a race, this is not a sprint; it's the most exacting marathon any human being can undertake.

This journey is best approached in a manner that although the final goal of Moksha (liberation), is being sought and can be attained in a single life time, it may well be that this is not realistically achievable by virtue of the aspirant's current commitments.

So bearing this in mind; always be aware that even if the final goal is not achieved in this life time, you will be banking into the bank of good karma; you will also be preparing the ground to be born into circumstances (in your next incarnation), so as to continue this journey and eventual consummation of the final great path. Of course there is always the possibility that you may be graced with Moksha when leaving your human form. This possibility has been documented by the Avatar Mother Meera, as her uncle Reddy and constant aid, attained Moksha at the moment of passing over.

Questions and answers

This little note was given to the student after helping the Master with a task. It shows the great humility of the Master:

A friend is there for you, always
Come night come day
When things are good, when things are bad
When you are happy when you are sad
A friend is for life, a Divine blessing from Paramatman
A jewel beyond material wealth
Thank you for being that friend

Blessings always – Deus

The Master gives a note to one of his female students:
Master: My dearest devotee, as long as you need me, I will be here for you, you are protected and loved.
See me each and every day, in the sun, the stars, the grass, the birds, for I am all that there is.

The Teacher, warm and friendly, dignified and courteous, is always ready to encourage:

Master: Welcome to the brotherhood/sisterhood my friend, keep the questions coming, and gather more light.
I was here before the beginning of time and will be here forever after.
Your teacher and guide always

"TAT TVAM ASI". Deus – OM SHIVO HAM

Q. Master, how should we conduct ourselves in this world?
Master: One must *discriminate* between good and bad (skilful or unskilful), mankind (you), have that choice; ask yourself am I serving my ego or my soul? Kindness and love will advance your soul/spirit.

Be as I, in this world but not of it, do not resent obstacles, but realise that they strengthen us. How can God reveal himself to a seeker who sticks to his regular routine of luxury?

Learn to live in both worlds, spiritual and the world of life and form, both are Paramatman [Paramatman translates as the supreme ultimate God].

You are on The Final Great Path at last, keep a steady momentum, see God in everything, I am very pleased with all your hard work and effort, continue in this manner but do not overdo it.

OM
My blessings always; Deus and beyond

Q. The student asks the Master if he minds all the questions being posed to him:
Master: The spirit of enquiry will unfailingly lead to oneness (non - dualism).

Q. Master, at times I feel discouraged and tired of walking the final great path, I find it hard to understand you:
Master: Take one step toward me and I will take one hundred towards you. Do not try to understand me for it is not possible, I am one with Paramatman.

True values are dependent on neither poverty nor wealth, both are illusory. God's gift of nature is free to all, the sound of birds singing, the smell of the grass; the sight of the rising sun. Look for all of God's gifts and add to the one I have given you.

Wherever we are placed in the world we can practice the path of peace, love and harmony, the empty hand is peace.

You have free will, if at any time you feel you no longer wish to aspire, that is fine, there is never a step lost.

Do not try to understand me as this isn't possible for the human mind.

Q. Here the student has questioned the wisdom of the Master's instruction.

Often the master will ask a student to change their practice or to carry out an action. The action is never contrary to the teachings which have the supreme foundation of Divine love, but at times these requests may seem strange to the conditioned human mind.

Sitting behind these requests is a test or rather a check by the master on the student's willingness to relinquish free will. At the end of the day, the truth is that it was our request before incarnating to be allowed free will. It is precisely free will that allowed the ego so much scope and in so doing the ego grew and grew to astronomical proportions:

Master: If you wish to learn my science and my way, let the teacher be the needle, let the student be the thread and practice unremittingly.

If you do not pursue the path to its consummation, then a little bit of crookedness in the mind may turn into a major warp, please reflect on this.

Each time a student starts to feel down and approaches the Master, further encouragement is always given. In most cases the Master will watch and wait for his student to make the first approach, but occasionally will pre-empt the problem arising.

Master: My devotee, you were once one with the Divine, if it is your wish to regain that place whilst still in human form, then you must continue to put in with Prayer, Jappa Mantra, and Devotion.

Offer all to God, food, the air you breathe, your good health. Thank the Divine for your many blessings.

Gently drop Divine Holy Mother Meera and devote yourself and your thoughts to Paramatman, there is nothing that is not the Divine.

Have courage, hang in, be resolute in your wants and want the Divine.

Pray direct now to the Divine – ask *who am I, who am I?* Pause and wait for the answer, again pray; "by your grace Holy Father please reveal to me the secret (keep on even before sleep)." End all useless mind activity, be ever so humble. Pray, Paramatman, I am thy child, please reveal thyself.

Authors note:

For most aspirants there are no tangible signs of progress, some start to expect visions, out of body experiences or some other spectacular occurrence. So when these do not materialise they get disillusioned, this disillusionment can become quite compounded over the years. This frustration will usually magnify the ego; the student can even start to manifest anger. These negative attributes are the very things we need to deal with, to overcome them, to disentangle ourselves from.

So, although it seems as if nothing is happening, the very processes of transformation are in fact taking place. Some recognise these ego traits far quicker than others and find a way to negate them. Others can get into a vicious circle were the same situations continue to manifest. If this happens take time out to contemplate on why this is so. From there act to reduce & minimalize future occurrences – remember the ego will do all it can to stop you.

One of the devotee's has difficulty with frustration, becoming angry and impatient for results.

Master: The nearer you become to myself and mother Meera, the harder your ego will try and claim you, offer everything to me, to Meera, to the Divine.

My dear devotee, thank you for giving your anger to me, now give me your life, everything you do, do it in my name, my Bhakti Yogi.

I will always be for you my son, just say my name and allow me to slowly bring you back to me, for I am the Divine.

Authors note:

Now then, this is very, very important, "Now give me your life", the master requests. This on the face of it sounds very much like the leader of many a cult movement; oh boy does this sound dangerous.

Over many, many years, I slowly became aware of the master's subtle tests/checks, I was applying my own observations in order to answer the very possibility of being drawn, unsuspected, into a sinister cult, certain internal questions needed to be resolved.

Over all the years I have been taught by the master, I asked myself, what has he gained? The absolute truth is nothing, nothing financially, nothing materially and absolutely nothing regarding control. His circumstances (living in the world as a householder and as a family man), haven't changed one little bit. If anything, the human side to his life is far more difficult ever since he retired from work having to make ends meet on a state pension.

OK, this being the case, what exactly are his teachings? Is he trying to get us to turn our backs on the everyday world? Are his teachings radical? Do his teachings result in conflict and strife? Do his teachings promote hate? Is he asking for sons and daughters to leave their families? The answer to all these questions is an emphatic no.

Looking deeper into what, in fact, I have gained from his teachings, really tells the story. I have been given the keys to the Kingdom of Heaven, I have been given the method and means to unravel the Gordian knot of my conditioning, and providing I continue to follow these teachings I will attain to self-realization and the acquisition of total peace and supreme bliss and happiness. My check list revealed my master stands to gain nothing, I stand to gain everything...not really the attributes of a sinister cult leader is it.

Here the Master gives guidance relating to the path of the Bhakti Yogi, the path of love and devotion.

Master: My dear Bhakti Yogi and devotee, the more we know the better we forgive, whoever feels deeply feels for all whom live.

Peace, like charity, begins at home. You never lose by loving you always lose by holding back. Those who bring sunshine into the lives of others cannot keep it from themselves.

Every time you blink this is a miracle. To hear a baby cry, to see a bird, all we take for granted.

Your good Karma has allowed so much, don't miss it. Yes the final truth is subtle as are my many ways. Yes I will take you all the way, work harder on temper.

Learn to discriminate your chattering monkey mind and random thoughts, keep a tight reign. My devotee may God be with you, as I am every second.

Thank you so much, for being my friend.

Wisdom note:

"To give is life, to withhold is death." Deus

The Master advises that all the students should encourage and support each other; the Final Great Path can be like a giant roller coaster, many highs, many lows and many ups and downs.

Master: It is important now that you stick together; I would like you to take on the responsibility of bringing my devotees together for none of you are strong enough to go it alone.

Birds of a feather flock together, try to keep Divine Company whenever and wherever you can, this will aid in your ascension.

You are all moving very rapidly now, keep pushing, keep striving; don't give up now.

The master gives a warning of how far the ego will go to stop your quest.

Master: The Ego is very cunning and will stop at nothing to prevent you from becoming realized. The ego does not want to die, it will even go as far as leading you to your own death so that it can reincarnate again.

Do not go head to head with the ego, you will lose, it is best to adopt a soft and gentle approach. Just say to the ego...thank you for bringing me this far but you're not needed now, so now you can rest.

Authors note:

A sublime master stroke by the Master, was to involve us in charity work. Initially I was resistant to the idea, but as he was the Master who only had my own wellbeing at heart, I just did. Over the years I grew into this selfless giving. Embracing selfless service diminishes the ego substantially.

The Master is explicit in this instruction, which leads to the ultimate, the ultimate being Moksha/liberation.

Master: Be in God and God in you, the more you focus on God the more the "I", the ego, will fall away and then you will know.

Emphasis is now placed on detachment; this is an extremely difficult thing to do. The ego has a lot of fun with this one.

Master: You must now start to withdraw from this material world, yes carry out your duties as a husband, a wife, house holder, at work etc. but whenever not engaged in your duties, be in the Divine.

Try to see God in everything; although the material world appears solid with much variety, all is light.

One of the Master's students enquires about meditation.

Master: A thirst for the infinite, for cosmic consciousness, for union with God, Paramatman or the absolute has possessed many minds in many cultures for thousands of years.

Meditation is pure awareness without thought. Eastern/Western meditation are different but with one single aim. Meditation can and does improve physical and mental health, principally by releasing stress; physiological and psychological changes take place.

The heart rate decreases by an average of three beats per minute. The rate of breath decreases. Blood lactate decreases. Alpha and Theta waves are produced from the brain.

Ten - Twenty minutes per day is fine. A poised posture is very helpful; Easy, Thunderbolt, Egyptian, Half Lotus and full Lotus are some but not absolute.

Meditation is a state of deep rest and relaxation. Once or twice a day is ideal; there are a great many methods of meditation; however, a good teacher is best, books are superb but not the best way to learn.

Meditation is sense withdrawal that turns your attention away from the bombardment of sense stimuli; so as to place attention on the object of meditation. One aim of meditation is to lift the consciousness to a state of pure consciousness (Samadhi).

It must be understood that having gained a good teacher one must put in to take out. You and you alone must put in the work. Do not deviate in any way if you are under instruction, you may feel nothing is happening but do carry on.

Psychic phenomena may take place, visions for example. *These must not become goals.* Also they may not be genuine mystical experiences, they will cause no harm so do not be alarmed if they occur. Meditation is, paradoxically, a doing that is yet a non-doing.

There is a plentiful supply of tranquil and meditative music available, prompting the student to ask this question.

Q. Can music help with meditation?
Master: Yes, certain types of music, use what inspires you, it will help you to forget body.

When meditating avoid getting angry or frustrated if thoughts or distractions come along, just smile inwardly and thank Paramatman for the test.

Authors note:

A few years ago, a friend of mine gave me a music disc, basically within the title was the word meditation; it was a compilation of Australian Aboriginal bush music.

Well I was sat in my chosen posture meditating, in the background was the steady drone of the Aborigine didgery-do, I was so relaxed, going deeper and deeper into my meditation...suddenly I found myself stuck to the ceiling! No not a mystical experience... a sudden loud screech had startled me making me jump out of my skin. It could have been a permanent out of body experience, for placed strategically within this compilation were animal sounds – the moral of the story – play your CD in a dry run before meditating.

Q. Master, how should we pray, and how long should we meditate for?
Master: When you pray do it with love and 100% effort, when you do meditation forget your body, out of each 24 hours give some time to yourself/soul/spirit, five minutes a day done with love and genuine effort is worth five hours done in the wrong frame of mind.

The master gives further instruction on praying thus encouraging the continual link.

Master: Keep asking and praying in this way; my dear Holy Mother Meera, thou art my Divine Spiritual Mother, I am thy child, please reveal thyself to me.
God, Holy Father, Paramatman, by your Divine Grace, please allow me instant realisation.
Thank you for the food I eat each day, for the water I drink, for the roof over my head, for the air I breathe, I take these for granted each and every day; Paramatman, may I also thank you for my present wonderful incarnation.

Paramatman I wish to ask and pray for world peace, to thank you for prayers from my teacher and intervention in Zaire, what happened was a Divine miracle, thank you dearest God. Please bless me that I may see ever more, please fill me with your light, pure white.

THE FINAL GREAT PATH

By your Grace I have opened, by your Grace may I become one with the light; with your Divine light. Please take me by the hand Divine Mother, Divine Father ever closer to Paramatman whilst I am still in a Human form, guide me ever onwards.

Here the Master warns us of the consequence of unskilful prayer, we have to be mindful of karma.

Master: Ask for everything from Paramatman, though be careful what you ask for as it may just be given, then you will have to bear. For example, you may ask to win the lottery, the next thing you know your life is in a complete mess, you lose friends, hundreds suddenly come begging, and you cannot handle the media interest etc.

The Master outlines the intricacies of Karma, the spiritual law of cause and effect.
Master: Most doctrines of karma are incomplete; the fundamental law of karma is governed by *intent*, for example. A man is driving his car to work and a cyclist suddenly pulls out in front of the car, he swerves to miss it and in so doing crashes into another car killing the driver.
His intent was to avoid hurting the cyclist, he did not intend to kill the other driver; he was nothing more than a vehicle for the Divine law of karma. So, he did not accrue unskilful karma, he accrued skilful karma for trying not to hurt anyone. There was also a woman who witnessed all this, so it was the karma of the dead driver to die in this way, it was also the karma of the bystander and the driver who swerved to be traumatised in this way, the law of karma is exact.

This comment by the master was made during a conversation on so called Holy wars.

Master: It is truly disgusting that humanity kills each other in the name of God; God would never have a human kill another human being.

Here, one of the Master's students is in crisis, this happens to all at some stage of the path, in fact crisis can come many times in many and varied forms.
It usually arrives after an abrupt karmic payback, but as you progress toward that final goal the ego throws as many obstacles on the path as it can muster e.g.

115

doubt, uncertainty, a feeling of unworthiness, futility, habits that seem impossible to break.

It may seem at times that the world is conspiring to prevent you from realization; it is at these times that it's so easy to blame God for your situation. Whenever this sort of thing happens I get a mental image of Basil Fawlty (John Cleese in the Fawlty Towers comedy series), shaking that branch in the air as he looks up heavenward shouting, "Thank you so bloody much God," because his car had broken down, he then proceeds to beat his car with the branch, wonderful.

Master: Accept your humanness, try not to get upset. Pray – lead me O God Divine from the unreal to the real, from darkness to light, from death to immortality.

Say to yourself whenever negativity creeps in, I am not afraid; I have every confidence in myself, every day in every way I am getting better and better.

My dear friend and devotee, please do not question me but revert back to Divine mother Meera - for the moment (believe), you are making excellent progress and will continue to do so as long as you have implicit trust in me.

Believe in yourself and gently push the barriers away. Om Namo Bhagavata Mater Meera (jappa mantra), use it! Om Namo Bhagavata Amma Meera, use it! Jai Amma Meera, use it! Om Namo Shivaya (one with God), use it! Use the beads. Believe in me for I am one with Paramatman.

I will tread the path with you; I will carry you when you are weary; I will be with you when you need me, all you need is simple belief in me.

Here, the Master's emphasis is on awareness.

Master: "Awareness", now there's a sweet little word.

I want you to keep repeating to yourself whenever you are not engaged in your worldly duties; "I am one with God", then a few months later to move on from that affirmation to, "One with God", then again a few months later moving on to, "with God", and then finally to, "God".

Look for God in everything; let the scales drop from your eyes.

You are *IN* God and one with.

I brush close past you, but you do not yet see...

THE FINAL GREAT PATH

Authors note:

It is very useful when you are on your own to just look at and even touch things around you as internally you say to yourself, this isn't real, it's God, just an illusion, all atoms, all particles just vibrating at different rates.

All of the Master's students continually look for explanations within the confines of temporal expression.

Master: It is fine on this level to be involved in concepts, e.g. tea, sugar, Sadhana, mudra, religion, football match etc. but at some stage concepts have to be left behind as your consciousness rises, then all just is.

The devotee asks the difference between certainty and faith.
Faith is a bridge between uncertainty and certainty, certainty is when one day your consciousness just goes whoosh! And you just know.
The Master gives instruction on seeing through Maya, illusion.

Master: I would like you to gaze gently at those trees and see if you can see beyond their form.
I would like you whenever you can, even if it be a hundred times or more to gaze at me and try to see beyond my physical form. Then once seeing the Divine, see God behind all manifested form.
Learn to love the world, love all in it, it's you anyway; if you did not exist, none of this could exist.

Authors note:

When gazing it is very much a focusing non-focus, almost a trance state, that which you are focusing on may start to pulse, may start to brighten and light may start to emanate from the periphery of that which you are concentrating on, do not be alarmed when this light becomes ever brighter and all consuming.
A question is put to the Master if there is a way to the Divine for the mind that does not accept God or the Divine.

Master: An old Zen practice was to just sit and stare at a wall for hours, days, months, years, until one day the wall just disappears and all just is...reality reveals itself.

But the way of Zen is extremely difficult; it is like climbing the north face of the Eiger without provision.

Yes, I know the path is difficult but the harder you work you become the path for others to follow including your family; a most worthy task.

Already you are carrying out Meera's and my work for which I thank you. Our path will spiral ever upward as your realisation grows. Although it is your life and you may stop at any time, you must never ever feel obligated.

As of now you are one with Paramatman, a time will come when you are the Divine.

I am here with you now and will stay with you as long as you wish my company. 'My devotee...a thousand times, thank you.'

Authors note:

After many years of striving, a strange phenomenon manifested. Frequently on coming out of meditation, I would take my time (as one should), in returning to normal human consciousness. On opening my eyes I would just casually look at the carpet in front of me and the carpet would begin to shimmer and vibrate – revealing what seemed to be dancing atoms...

Again, the Master reminds his student to move away from identification with the earthly vehicle. Many times does the Master draw a parallel to the body and getting into a car to drive it; in the same way the soul drives the vehicle of the body.

The master is also pointing out the importance of the human mind, for what we think and feel today we become tomorrow.

Master: You must realise that you are more than just human, if you allow your mind to limit your awareness to just your human condition you will be restricting yourself from the truth.

You are spiritual beings on a material journey, not material beings on a spiritual journey.

The emphasis is now being placed on affirmation as the human mind slips so readily into the old habitual traits.

Master: You must realise, you are not the body, the body is just a vehicle – you are a being of light, never born, never dying, eternal and immortal.

I want you to keep telling yourself – I am an actor playing the part of a Butler. But over many centuries I have played the part of the Butler so well that I have over identified with this role, believing that I am the Butler. Yet the truth is that I am a being of light, eternal and immortal, never born, never dying.

The mind is a product of the brain's activity which is organising all sense stimulation. Of course, we now know that what is being reported by the five senses is illusory, so another tool is introduced to help train the restless mind.

Master: I would like you now to repeat the mantra you have been given whenever you can apart from when you go to the bathroom out of respect.

Eventually for some, unusual phenomena begin to manifest.

Q. What is that misty tingling sensation we feel around our heads?
Master: That is God's omnipresence.
.
Q. What is that tingling sensation in the middle of the forehead between the eyebrows?
Master: That is God's Divine light entering what is known as the Ajna Chakra or third eye.

The devotee enquires as to what happens when we die.

Master: In most cases you would go straight to the astral plane, if the last thing you are thinking of for example is your departed mother, then it would be your mother who you would meet; if it were Krishna, Jesus, Allah, Meera, Baba etc. that's who you would meet. If you truly wish to meet God your last thought before passing over must be very powerful; have an unshakable focus on God.

Q. What happens then?
Master: You would then reside in a part of the astral consistent with your karma, if you have been a loving; caring and giving person you will be with likeminded people.

Q. How long do we spend on the astral plane and where do we go from there?
Master: On average about fifty years, you then go through a second death in order to be reincarnated here on earth again. This second death is nowhere near as traumatic as the one here; you are given help on the astral. If you are on the final great path, when you pass over do not be satisfied with just occupying the

astral plane, push through to ever higher and greater planes. Do not ever stop; you are only as limited as you allow your mind to limit you.

Q. Master, I have heard there is a technique for going back to previous incarnations, could you teach me?

Master: To go into your past lives would serve no purpose; it may only go to upset you as there may be very unskilful words, actions and deeds in your previous lives. But us coming together in this incarnation is not by accident, just think of all the little intricacies that went into us coming together, without just one of those it would not have happened.

The Master reassures the student of continual guidance.

Master: An Avatar will always be with you, even when the physical body is not, and will be now for all eternity.

Look for God in everybody's heart for God is there, all have God consciousness in their hearts.

Here the devotee asks a very important question regarding the difference between an Avatar and an Avadhutta.

Master: The difference between an Avatar and an Avadhutta is that an Avatar comes directly from God; an Avatar is God taking a human form in order to communicate directly to the human race. A human being can only aspire to that knowledge, but a human being can never attain to the full extent of God while in human form.

There is a big difference between self-realisation and God realisation, God realisation may occur when your earthly vehicle, the body stops functioning, and you pass over, but cannot be attained while still in human form.

The Chakras only exist within the human form, for this reason, self-realization can only be attained in a human body. A self-realised human being is known as an Avadhutta, a pure one, one who sees and knows all to be the Divine, who sees through this Maya (illusion).

A human Guru/Teacher can never lead you all the way, only part the way, only God or an Avatar can lead you all the way.

Q. Does an Avatar have to be incarnate to lead their devotees to the ultimate consummation of the final great path?

Master: No, an Avatar is always present, always eternal, will always be there to guide, e.g. Jesus is an Avatar, he is not incarnate but will lead all his devotees regardless.

If you do not follow an Avatar, go direct to God, to Paramatman, God will guide you.

One of the devotees is puzzled as to why the Master wishes to remain anonymous.

Master: I live as a householder in order to show you that the Divine life can be lived regardless of your circumstances. As I live as a householder, therefore I must taste the fruits of the tree of the world, I also weep at suffering and inhumanity. Please retain your faith in myself and mother Meera.

The Master now reveals how the continued connection with the Divine, will change your rate of vibration.

Q. How will we know that the teaching we dispense is correct for that individual?

Master: Pray for guidance, offer the teaching up to the Avatar, the Avatar is with you always now, and then what you teach will be right, for the Avatar will be guiding you. Pray as much as you can; ask for world peace; ask for self-realisation; ask to be able to see ever more; ask for God to reveal his celestial form. Talk to God as much as you can; when not praying or talking to God (Paramatman, the Supreme, to Krishna, Jesus, Mary, Baba, Meera, Allah etc.), or whoever is your chosen deity, do mantra, focus constantly on the Divine. Whenever you are doing mantra, repetition of Divine names, the Divine vibration will pour from you. I am with you now, from now until eternity, until the final consummation of the final great path, until we merge at the end.

A gifted student presented the Master with one of his stories so designed to teach and convey a spiritual message.

Master: My devotee, you have a very good style of writing, your human understanding of the Divine is very far removed from most on this planet, as many people as possible should be able to read this vision of yours.

Please allow yourself to continue to expand, be just light, cool and clear, without colour.

Allow yourself to be one with me, the universe, the stars, the oceans, one with all, ever expanding, radiate love, expound love and expand.

121

As you say, you were one with the Divine but took human form, you/we/humanity were arrogant and were certain you would not forget your true nature...you did.

I am much more than your closest friend, I am here to guide you back, please do not get caught up in who is who, for it's a trap set by the ego.

Your Divine friend who ever was and ever will be.

Further guidance and encouragement is given to the Bhakti Yogi who has also become a teacher.

Master: My very dear Swami,

Thank you for all the tasks you take on for me, you are now well into your destiny.

Never ever fear for I am always with you, guiding your heart and your feet, a teacher you were born to be, I have waited a long time for you. Feel no pressure; however, you will always have your free will.

Divine Mother Meera, Sweet Mother and I will give all the help you will need.

Love, love, love, Divine love and Paramatman light will speed up the spiritual growth required.

"*Focus, Aspiration, Affirmation.*" Teach these for me as we get ever closer to the Golden Yuga.

Please do not ever allow yourself to lose the precious reality of who I am; your awareness is now your final path. Here for you always.

TAT TVAM ASI

CHAPTER 10

THE KNOWLEDGE IN FOCUS

The following are questions that have been grouped under headings. Under each heading is a selection of answers that underpin and elucidate that particular topic.

BEING A TEACHER

A student who has been under the tutelage of the master for many years has been asked to write a book on the Master's teaching, but he has many doubts as he knows he hasn't attained to Moksha at the time of asking.

1. I will work through you and with you, the book will help. No, you will not need to be realized. You must know beyond all knowing that the Divine is with you; the work is very important.

Please keep asking. Your aspiration for me must be as needed as the air you breathe. All is me. (YOU), you have got to come to this realization. You still let the Maya fool you. Use all of the illusion, stop, take stock and see me for there is only *me.*

2. Bend and lift all that are low is the best form of exercise for us. Teach a man to fish and he eats for life.

Keep yearning for the Divine. Want the Divine mother, she is your mother.

3. Swami, I am here to teach you, and to be a very close friend, I will never leave you. The teachings will continue.

Please lead a nice life that gives you pleasure but also is of a vast spiritual nature. Want the Divine each and every day. Want Meera, want me as Deus; want Krishna.

GNOSIS

Here the Master imparts knowledge.

1. All humans operate through consciousness, sub consciousness and super-consciousness. My wish for you is realization, then on to Divine consciousness. You can and will do it, for you are at a stage where all is possible with my help; that you will always have.

Swami, the state of the world is as the majority want it; correct for the moment, it is going to change. Change must come but it requires our help.

2. Advaita means non dualism, to try and gradually see all as the Divine. You know the truth from an intellectual point of view, I now need you to try and see my teaching to you, no subject or object, all just is from a Zen point of view. There is not hot nor cold, no male nor female, everything, just is. The human mind is like a mad monkey, it makes things up for it likes to be diverse.

From your standpoint as one with the Divine...all just is. All you see is just you, vibrating at slower and slower speeds – but still you.

Ice is water, yet it can also be steam and it can be its original form of water. It can drive water engines (h2o), yet it is still water.

All that your senses tell you is the Divine – Advaita – just one. A diamond is coal, yet as a diamond it will cut anything on your planet – All is one – One is all; you and all your body parts are one.

Only the mind puts a block on what you are capable of, however look at intent before you do anything. Desire to merge with me once more, remember all is the Divine, the Divine is all; there is no more; you have got to come to this realization.

KARMA

The aspirant enquires as to what happens to a person who has taken their own life.

1. Swami, Now is the time for you to push the barriers. See the Divine in all that is created. Look for the Atman in all people, good and bad, for the Atman is the same in all humans.

All human life forms are born with free will, the life is yours. If one is ill and wishes to take it, that is up to them; they will incur no karma for taking an own life. The karma will be based on the life they led prior to the second of extinction. The part of the astral they go to will be based on the final count of karma and based on the law of attraction.

A person who takes their own life comes back very quick, usually within one year, again based on karma. If the karma is really bad, the comeback time is even quicker.

If the person has given a lot of their life to an Avatar in love and prayer and at the last few seconds of life they aspire with all their heart to come to the Avatar, then yes, they will come to the Avatar. The final aspiration must be as one great last thought.

2. An aspirant enquires about occult teachings

Swami, yes, last night exited me also; it was superb to be a part of all that went on. The joy on people's faces was a great joy to me also; I am and was so impressed with the entire evening.

The final path does not use such childish and very dangerous games as you express in your letter. Yes, astral travel is a massive help to realise the soul does not die. Yes, the other practises you mention can lead to insanity, but the worst thing is they lead one to the left hand path; one is then committed to untold horror and the correct karma. Your answer must be short and blunt..."do not even think about it". There are better ways to waste one's life.

Thank you for my beloved present and all you do for me.

Continue to want the Divine and only the Divine; this is your final goal. Grow each day into the Divine, this is your right.

3. Swami, Wow! You are indeed me and I am you. Close the gap; push for the truth, all is an illusion for all is the Divine.

Demons are a product of the human mind. As such they have the intelligence of the humans producing them. If he intends to have any control on them, he will be in serious trouble. They are beyond his conception and will give him terrible grief. Should he take this silly path I will not bail him out, the karma has to be paid. Should I help him, it will still have to be paid, an endless wheel of karma.

Positive thoughts for you Swami: Lead me from the darkness to the light, from the unreal to the real, from death to immortality. Get to grips with whom and what you really are. Bask in the truth.

Authors note:

For many years I studied various aspects of occult teachings, from oriental Tantra to western Enochian magic, which included the evocation of spirits and demons through the use of ritual & vocalising what is termed barbaric names.

This study was purely to arrive at a comprehensive knowledge of the various practices being used to communicate with the spiritual realm. I perceived that this knowledge would place me in a position of strength in making correct decisions in my search for the truth.

It has to be said, that right from the moment of discovering these practices I was very uncomfortable with the idea, so never at any point did I attempt these dubious practices...anybody reading these pages who may be considering such a path please think again.

4. Swami, what a superb question to start the day with.

Your question: What you sow, you reap; what you give you receive; whatever is done, both good and bad you will get back, receive in this life or another.

Birth believe it or not is the result of karma, when you have been born and take a human body, male or female, it is down to you; karma is karma. First one must offer all actions to God, the Divine in truth, honesty and humility.

If you do bad actions you will receive bad karma, if on the other hand you do good actions you will receive good karma.

But then all humans have free will. One must come to a realization that one is being stupid and make changes. Very simply Swami what one thinks one becomes.

Even the worst idiots in the world will one day get fed up with the way of life they are living and try and seek out some answers. Karma as you suggest is not permanent, it can be changed by each and every human. However having free will they must first of all desire a change.

Mother, other Avatars and I also take this task upon ourselves to help all we can, however we will never interfere with free will in humans. But no! Poor karma is not eternal.

Humanity will never be doomed for humanity is very dear to the Divine and will not allow total stupidity to last forever. Mankind must however do some of the work itself. It must make the leap of faith.

5. Mankind must find the source of his ignorance to break the cycle; you under-estimate mankind. The cycle of karma can and will be changed by man for mankind, the change however must be wanted.

There will come a time in each person's life where he/she will crave a change and will want it more than life itself. The Divine will be there to help when this happens, the cycle is not eternal – nothing in your world is

6. If man accepts his karma it will prevail, he must be prepared to open up to change, it is of no use throwing your hands in the air and moaning. Pray to the Divine for help, for insight. As I have said offer all, good and bad, to the Divine. It can be stopped but man must do something, must accept that he and he alone has brought this on himself. Man must want a change and seek Divine help.

Look very deep into Mother Meera's book, Answers. The answer you seek is there.

Authors note:

With respect to Karma, although I fully appreciated the workings of this law it began to baffle me in this way – if for example I intentionally hit someone, in time I would also be hit. But this would mean that the person hitting me would then have to be hit and so it would go on. So how on earth can this cycle be broken, if indeed it can? If it can't be broken then the human race is doomed, war begets war; murder begets murder and so on; at least that was what I had reasoned.

The cycle of karma can be broken in a couple of ways:

Although I may intentionally hit someone and let's say broke their nose, this Karma could be visited upon me by someone accidentally hitting me in the nose and breaking it; mine was done with intent, the other not.

By the intervention of Divine grace. Only by the most sincere regret and by the will to do nothing but good; backed up with ardent and powerful prayer for forgiveness will this be granted. But it has to be sincere and backed up with action – God, don't forget, is omniscient and omnipotent and can't be conned.

EGO

1. Only the ego is deluded. It thinks it is an "I" and it lives in a unit/a body that believes it. There is only the Divine, nothing else exists; all is one. My Divine love to you and all the work you do for me. Want to be one with me as much as I want you back. However, do not miss this glorious human life; just learn to discriminate. Tread with care.

2. Swami, we are one with the Divine, do not ever forget this. Even I yearn to return and be free of my earth responsibilities. Whilst I am here I work 24/7. You are my finest student and devotee this time. I salute you Swami. This is for the real you not your ego. Keep a tight hold on it.

Authors note:

The praise given by the Master here could be quite tricky to deal with as the ego is ever ready to pounce; this presents the ego with an opportunity to become

127

puffed up and inflated...The ego is dealt with by humility and the cultivation of detachment and the continued application of Focus, affirmation and aspiration.

Another invaluable way of eradicating the ego is through selfless service. This is something I found hard to come to terms with, the difficulty for me was my conditioning, indeed the difficulty that's faced by most of us.

You see we are brought up to be very competitive, to fight for what you want – it breeds selfishness; and yet this competitive edge isn't natural to us. If you observe little children together playing, in most cases they are kind, considerate, caring and giving.

Back in 2003 my master ran an idea past me, what do you think about raising money for Just a Drop, a charity who provide clean drinking water for children world-wide. Although, I have to say, this didn't appeal to me because of my conditioning, I embraced it as I understood that whatever the master would suggest was always in the interest of his students, it had a profound effect upon me. I spoke to the founder of our martial arts system, who agreed this to be a wonderful and noble cause.

Over the years we have raised thousands of pounds thereby bringing clean drinking water to various locations around the world, bringing life to thousands who would have otherwise died. If I were to depart this world today, I would feel it has been a worthwhile incarnation just by virtue of saving these lives. Walking the final great path and helping others along the way gives purpose to this life – it bestows, in a humble manner, a beautiful warm glow to the heart.

Giving and helping doesn't have to be financial, just giving some of your time to others, to listen to their problems, to be a shoulder to cry on. Giving kind words, giving encouragement – being kind, considerate and loving, a hug here, and a gentle touch there, all go toward selfless service; because all of this is in the interest of others, not yourself, it's all non-ego.

Help extended to others can come from your own difficult and painful experiences. One example of this is when losing a loved one, a relative, a friend, a much-loved pet. By cultivating, in due course, coping mechanisms to come through the darkness; we are enabling ourselves to relate to and help others come through their tough times.

3. Keep in mind that you are one with the Divine – were once conscious of the Divine and will one day be again the Divine. You and you alone must want this very badly. You must aspire each and every day to this but in a nice happy way, no pressure. Have a foot in each world...yours and the Divine; learn to bear both worlds, try not to judge. The ego is for this world...the non-ego for the Divine

world, you decide. You were given free will which will never be taken away, it is now yours to deal with...I will guide you until you say stop.

I was here before the start; I will still be here when all is finished. This being the case so was you, the real you...not James, come on! You know who and what you are (eyes open), push each and every day, aspire to the Divine.

4. To bow to the lotus feet of a great teacher or Avatar, is an invocation, an endearment, a love of the Divine. It's the ability to bring ones ego under control to bow to the feet of the Divine in human form.

In the west it is unthinkable to bow to the feet of another human. The only reason you bow to my feet and Mothers is so that we can touch your temples in Darshan and Pranam.

We do not wish you to bow to us for any other reason; we are beyond ego. If you wish to bow out of love and respect for the Divine then that is fine, we do not expect you to bow to us.

In Asia/India it is their way to show humility and non-ego. All I wish from either of you is friendship and trust, you show me both, I want nothing more.

Let go of ego, draw closer to God, I only wish you to dissolve back into originality, to once again be one with me. To remain on earth is a silly game. To believe this illusion true reality is for children, the only reality is the Divine.

5. Am delighted that you are yearning for the Divine more and more; there comes a time in life when the pull gets stronger. Just simply see that all is the Divine. There is not one atom in any part of the universe that is not God, gross atoms and fine atoms alike are the Divine, the ego wishes humans to think otherwise, the ego wants total control. You owe the ego nothing for what has the ego ever done for you but bring you grief? You were, are and always will be "*One*" with the Divine.

Each time you open your eyes, see me. I am all there is, therefore you are all there is, not the host, not James, but the God within.

My time is your time, I will always be with you, I will always guide you. Your progress in life has been little short of a time warp, you are on a massive leap home at quantum speed.

Have a superb weekend.

6. Your wish is my command. You have asked that I do not let you go, so be it. You and the Divine are one, drop the "I" and see the truth, the reality and not the perceived reality.

Drop all the conditioning that has been heaped upon you. You and the Divine are one. Of all life forms, you (human), are the nearest to your original self. The

Atman is the final bridge. Want the Divine as you want air (Save this and keep coming back on it).

7. Forget where the sound comes from [during meditation I began hearing the sound of bells], this is ego trying to keep you bound to the senses. The sound is real, activated by meditation. Your consciousness is expanding and you will see and hear sounds and sights beyond your normal conceptual senses. Do not get too affixed to the sound or any experiences you have as it will become an ego trap preventing you from further growth, enjoy and ask for more, never stop your quest, never rest.

MAYA/ILLUSION

1. How are you to-day? You have had a lot of very active days. Weather is a bit odd, sun, rain, showers, to you and me, just a changing aspect of the "DOW," it will do what it is intended to do.

In the end all is the Divine and we as humans are not here to experience it anyway; all is Maya, do not get lost in the illusion.

2. As I have said before you must learn to live in both worlds, the Divine is the real one. Your journey is closing, see beyond the Maya for all that you see, hear, touch, taste and see is really the Divine, there is nothing else, there never was and there never will be.

Live in the moment of each day, embrace each day, but want the Divine. Help me to help the world, pray for world peace; pray to be a perfect glowing instrument that I may work through.

Know that I and all the Avatars are helping you, be open to our light. It/you will get brighter and brighter. Look for more to join us; they will be attracted to your light. All Swamis and Gurus give off light.

3. I am delighted that you decided to be a doer, you are a Divine teacher now and my blessings are upon you. Thank you for this generation and the generation to come. These are all God's children and they are very lost in the delusion of Maya, and of course very clever people conditioning them to their will. Civilisation is breaking down big time; yes I have it in hand...at the moment I am just allowing enough rope.

4. Everything you see is me, I am behind the illusion, look hard for me. I will protect your sight from the blaze of light so have no fears. Your best friend is the Divine.

5. All is the Divine...the Divine is all, see the truth, not what your mind wishes you to believe, Maya is Maya. The illusion keeps one bound to the wheel of life. You are doing so well, keep a nice steady constant pressure on.

THE FINAL GREAT PATH

6. Keep looking for me in all that you see. I am pure colourless light and yet all colours, all lights. Push to see me, bother me, keep asking to see me, there is nothing else, only me, all else is a creation of your mind (Maya).

LOVE

1. Nothing that you ask me is daft, I am here for you. If you are asking love of the Divine (Bhakti) then offer all you have. If you refer to human love this means to love a human more than you love yourself, most people mix love up with lust. The ego is very clever at crossing the line either way. Real love is to come last to the person that you claim to love.

Author's note:

It is now obvious, that this last statement is the meaning behind Jesus's statement: *"Those who are first shall be last, and those who are last shall be first."* This statement is also a question of humility.

2. My dear Swami, your faith and love has brought you a long way. Please keep up your amazing progress, not for me, but for you.

3. Yes all that I do as teacher is for you. You are all still asleep and you gave me the power to do as necessary to wake you all up, I do this with love and honour.

You will learn trust beyond your wildest dreams, and you will move to-ward home much quicker. Yes, I am your very dear friend, but above all I am the Divine.

My love for you all is my motivation to bringing you back and allowing you knowledge that most will only dream of. All I ask of you all is to extend your love, and roll my eternal teachings out to those who are ready. You will know who is ready. You still have and will always have free will. Mother and I need your help, of course nothing will stop our work but we would just love you to be involved.

4. Sin comes about by not loving enough, real genuine love which means not wanting a thing in return.

5. Humans do not love the Divine. One must love the Divine without expectation; total surrender must be given for real love is to love the Divine. One must love with sincerity and conviction; the love has to be genuine.

6. You are merging every day to me. I am the ocean, dive in and enjoy the love and comfort of the Divine; the eternal love and warmth of the creator.

7. The Lotus is unfolding for the benefit of Mankind. The light is getting brighter and brighter, soon it will be a superb brilliance that engulfs the world. Our work is being done here on earth as it is in heaven. It has been a good time for me to come back.

MEDITATION

1. The four stages are BETA, ALPHA, THETA AND DELTA; the last two do not come into play for a long time. There is a fifth stage that of Gamma, but here the mind is in overdrive.

Alpha is the most important one; it gives peace to the body, mind and the soul. This is a stage required to reach Moksha, Nirvana; Samadhi.

Meditation must be for real, not a game. One must want to be realised; one must aspire to the Divine.

We can only take the horse to water; we cannot make the horse drink it; humans do not realize the miracle of having a teacher of your calibre with them.

You and I are now one, we work together for the sake of the blue planet and the life forms upon it; there is no longer a you or me we are now fused for all eternity.

2. Thank you so much for asking re my life. I work through an inferior medium, a body. I am under a massive workload at the moment as Deus; so much to be done. Please do not worry, all is under control.

Most religions have an inner sanctum; this is kept secret from the masses. Colour meditation and similar are used; there is no need to change this. It is one of many hundreds of ways of bringing the mind under control for the human mind is like a mad monkey leaping and jumping around, ever restless.

Colour meditation is safe and has no religious connotations. Everything that you do as a teacher is correct. All my teachings to you are not human, they are not fallible. As long as you and other teachers stay with the original, they will always be correct.

See me in all you do every day, I alone am behind your illusion.

3. Meditation and jappa mantra are the vital keys.

All starts with a thought, the computer you sit at was once a thought as was the desk it sits on, as was your world before God created it.

ASPIRATION

1. Swami, it's safe to open, aspire to me and me alone. The most important aspect of your life is the Divine, all else will follow.

2. Swami, I have just called in for post and to check Barney and check the house. As I say, I am cat and house sitting. It's so nice to hear from you.

Thank you for the document, it is very safe in my hands and will be seen by no one, nil, not a single soul; thank you for your trust.

Yes, your planet needs all the help it can get. Mother is working non-stop; Divine blessings to her.

We have moved a long way, now we will slow the pace down a bit, realization will come.

Remember all including you is one with the Divine; there is nothing that is not God. Every atom; sub atom; particle; vibration, keep this in mind and try not to sink to lower human thinking. Aspire to the Divine, keep at it, do not stop. The rewards are beyond your imagination. Aim ever upward, I am waiting for you.

3. Continue your deep want to be in the Divine. Let go slowly of your want to be immersed too much in the low physical world although, yes, it is fun to a point.

4. Swami, You came to earth to learn, *to find out who and what you are*...now you know. You have had the love and trust to follow a Master, the humility to act without question; to follow without question. As you know had I not wished you to find me then it would not have been possible.

You now stand on the pinnacle and it is now up to you, this could be your last or last but one incarnation. You do mine and Mothers work with love and pride.

Spend the rest of this life following us (If you wish), free will is yours; you will incur no unskilful karma by not following us. Aspire to the Divine at all possible chances but please live as a human. *Finding the Divine is a quest of great beauty, not a chore.*

This is of great importance, please save it. You are on the easy bit now, just simply want the Divine, and offer all to the Divine for there is nothing that is not the Divine. The computer in front of you is made up of my molecules, your entire world is. All is the Divine, see through the Maya (Now).

5. Live in this world, bear it, but want the Divine and only the Divine. Aspire with all your heart. Yes, you are closing the gap (rapidly).

6. Please keep a gentle pressure on your up and ever rising to the Divine. You must come to realize that you and the Divine are indeed one, there is nothing more to learn. You have come an awful long way and must continue to go ever

upward, each and every day aspire to the Divine for you are one with the Divine but you will have to put the work in; I will be waiting for you.

7.   Together we will help mankind to make the leap of faith to the ultimate Divine, I will not do all the work, mankind must also put in, and they must show their intent to once again be one with me.

FOCUS

1.   Hello and good morning. My blessings are upon you. Keep up your pursuit of the Divine, whatever else you do with your life this is the most important. I am with you and by your side, now and for ever. There is no time in reality.

2.   You are indeed becoming more and more one with the Divine each day. Yes, one has to work on it, and yes, it is worth the small human effort.

3.   It is easy as a human to be side tracked. Best plan is to just keep on a little, tread the middle path. Accept that the Divine is a reality and keep up a slow but decisive push for union. In reality there is only one mind and one vibration, we have reacted to give more scope to our oneness. There is nothing anywhere that is not the Divine (not you), your Atman is one with at all times.

You operate through three levels i.e. conscious, subconscious and super conscious; you wanted free will and it was given, and it will never be revoked. Enjoy a human life but chase the real you. Draw a line that you will not cross; put a limit on the free will that you have been granted.

You asked me to be your teacher; as such I will push, pull and do whatever it takes to bring you back to me, as per your wishes. If I do not do it this life time then I will do it next time but why wait? We will do it now. Just know in your deepest heart of hearts who and what you really are; then continue to help me and Ma with all other life forms.

You are a Swami (teacher), no less. You can and will do it. I am by your side.

AFFIRMATION

1. By your efforts, you are where you are. As you think, so you become; think you are one with the Divine at all times, act as though you are one with the Divine. All thoughts manifest, it is my way and cannot be changed, be careful what you think.

Wisdom note:

'Do not mistake this temporary abode as your eternal dwelling place. Do not lose heart at evanescent troubles and short-lived tragedies. Immerse yourselves in the effort to attain the eternal Lord. Everything in this world is subject to decay - if not today, sometime in the future.'

'It is not right to reject the Lord, who is eternally related to you, and be misled by this world with which one is connected to for a short while. Consider the number of births you have taken, the countless mothers, fathers, wives, husbands, sons, daughters, friends and enemies you've had.'

'Do they exist today? Do they remember the relationships? You are no one to them, and they are nobody to you. But you and they have the Lord in common as the unchanging relative. He is there throughout all births; He is eternal. He watches over you from one birth to another.'

'The Lord will never give you up. What greater tragedy can there be than forgetting such a Lord? With the senses weakened, powerless and refusing to function; with the parents, wife, children, and all relations crowding on one side; while the messengers of death compelling you to pack up for the journey without delay on the other side - who knows when this call will come and how? Before that moment comes, be ready with the thought of God.' Shri Satya Sai Baba

PART THREE

THE TEACHING

CHAPTER 11

THE PATH SPECIFIC

This section represents my personal experiential interpretation of the Master's guidance, a distillation and condensing his teaching; fundamentally a practical guide.

What is the final great path then? The goal of the final great path is Moksha; Moksha means liberation. It is the liberation from the endless cycle of reincarnation, of taking a body that is born and will die. It is the liberation from Maya (illusion). It is to reside in the place of "timelessness".

Each student who aspires to the final great path is likened to a lotus flower. The Lotus flower has been and still is a symbol of spiritual aspiration and will be found in many cultures around the world. It will be found most prominently in the architecture of ancient Egypt. It will be noted in the iconography of many other cultures, especially that of India.

The lotus flower starts its life at the bottom of the waters, covered and bogged down by all the silt and slime thereat. The aspiring students through their own effort, like the Lotus, will gradually pull themselves out of this silt and slime. As the lotus slowly and purposely rises out of the mud and into the waters, waters which slowly sooth and clean the slime from its petals, so it is with the student.

The lotus flower has just one mission in its life, that mission is to reach up and grow into the light above the waters.

The silt and slime represent our earthly bondage and conditioning to the sensual world; the waters represent the illusion of the material world; the light above the waters represent the Divine.

By the time the lotus flower rises out of the water and opens its petals, it is without blemish. The stains, the mud, slime and silt it thought to be part of its nature, thus feeling tarnished, have all been washed away. The lotus flower has grown into its true Divine nature, pure and perfect...as is the real non ego you.

Direction

I was brought up in one of the major faiths; I was taught that only the faith that I followed was the religion with all the truth. As I matured I began to question this assertion more and more. Why was/is there religious wars? Each religion is claiming to be the only true religion. I began a search for the common denominator in all religions, exoteric and esoteric alike. I spent many years searching and researching. Although there are many similarities between the various religions and philosophies, there is one simple common denominator between them all, and guess what it is, would you believe it... "GOD".

My conclusion was and is that GOD'S truth is there for all, regardless of race, colour or creed. This simple message is encrypted within the Great Pyramid, which you will meet with in the next part, focusing the heart and mind upon the Divine; it cuts through all dogma.

Many and varied are the rivers that flow to the sea of God, some twist and turn more than others, but all will eventually reach the sea. That which is offered here will accommodate all the various rivers. God will be found in the essence of the water particle, within the water particle is the essence of the great sea. We can all go directly to God.

Strong foundation

First and foremost, for the aspiring student is desire, the Aspirant must want the Divine.

There was a highly evolved Master, who was visited by a searcher of truth. The searcher pleaded with the master to impart the truth. The Master promptly rose from the seat and asked the searcher to follow. The Master made way to a river and asked the searcher to sit. As the searcher made to sit, the Master quickly seized the searcher and plunged the searcher's head under the waters. After a minute or two of the searcher struggling with the vice like grip, the master released the searcher. Coughing and spluttering the searcher enquired, `What'd you do that for, you nearly drowned me?` The Master replied, `*When you want the Divine as much as you wanted that breath of air, you will be ready to be taught.*`

Ideally the body should be kept strong and healthy, although for those with disability or illness there is what is known as Divine grace. The truth is, the human body "is" the temple of God; clearly identified as such by the Great Pyramid of Gizeh. Regardless of physical condition, press on and continue to climb your own inner holy mountain, the final great path is open to all. There is never a step along the final great path that is ever, ever lost.

There are many ways of keeping the body fit and healthy, here are just a few suggestions:

Swimming
Hatha Yoga
Tai Chi
Martial Arts (non-competitive)
Aerobics
Walking

With respect to Martial Arts, we state non-competitive as otherwise this would be ego building and could be detrimental in relation to Karma, of which more will be said shortly. I have been an exponent of the Martial Arts for many years, in the system of Zenyogkido (The Way of the Mind, Body and Spirit), it is stated, *"There is only one opponent to be defeated, and that is the self"*. Ego is by far the biggest obstacle to spiritual progress.

The path of the Bhakti Yogi (love & devotion – heart and mind), is the safest, no matter what religion you may follow, if indeed you follow one. No matter what name you may attribute to God, the path of Divine Love and devotion is a safe path.

The aspirant enquires of his master. `Master, why is faith so important upon this final great path? `

The Master replies. `Faith is the bridge between two shores, the shore of uncertainty, and the shore of certainty, now if you choose, go forth and build that bridge of faith to the shore of certainty, so that you too may arrive upon the shore of truth. `

The only foundation that will stand for eternity is that foundation that is built firmly upon the Divine.

CHAPTER 12

NOTHING HAPPENS BY ACCIDENT

There is what is known as the law of Karma, although for many people the suggestion of such a law is odious.

Karma in the west is touched upon by science in the theory put forward by Sir Isaac Newton, that of action – reaction, although this theory doesn't really go deep enough.

To illustrate the law of action – reaction, if you were to walk briskly past a lit candle, the flame would move. It is said that even a leaf falling from a tree has an effect on the world.

Karma in ancient Egypt was symbolised by the Goddess Maat. Maat represents universal truth, order and balance. The dead soul is oft represented in Egyptian hieroglyphs as a heart being weighed in one scale against an ostrich feather in the other. The wispy character of the ostrich feather meant it would be stirred by the slightest movement of air – it represented Karma. The heart of the deceased is being weighed by its environmental impact through thoughts, words and deeds.

Karma is firmly based on the belief/reality of reincarnation. Reincarnation happens by virtue of your real self, you are not your body; the human form is a vehicle for which your true self can experience the material world.

You are a spiritual being on a material journey, not a material being on a spiritual journey.

Your true self is the Soul/Spirit/Atman. The Soul/Spirit resides within your body, its location is within the middle of the forehead between the eyebrows known as the Ajna Chakra (Chakra is a Sanskrit term which means wheel), or third eye. We will come back to the topic of Chakras a little later. The Atman is external to the body and is located above the crown of the head. Your true self is the Atman; it is the soul that returns to a body by reincarnation. The soul is like the hard drive of a computer and records all of your thoughts, words, actions and deeds of your current and previous lives. At liberation the soul merges with the

Atman and the Atman then merges with Paramatman – the consummation of God realisation.

The human form is the highest conscious entity of God's creation, a human incarnation does not reincarnate into a lower form such as an animal or insect; it is only the human being that has an individual soul, all other species have a collective soul.

When I say the human form is the highest, it is not necessarily the most intelligent, for there are myriad other species throughout many Universes who are far more intelligent, but they don't have the conscious capacity for self and God realization.

The vast majority of humanity search without for our source, our beginning, but the Divine placed this knowledge in the last place most would search, in the middle of the forehead, between the eyebrows. Yeah I know, I can hear you now saying, `What! In the middle of the forehead – the guy's nuts.` This is exactly why it was placed there; no, not because I'm nuts.

As each body is fashioned/created by the Divine through childbirth, a soul/spirit becomes resident. The Atman, the real you, animates the soul and body but never incarnates.

During each incarnation of the Soul/Spirit (from here on the above terminology will be referred to as Soul), the thoughts, words, and deeds are banked so to speak, into two separate bank accounts, one positive and one negative, or using Buddhist terminology, one skilful and one unskilful.

The circumstances in which you find yourself now are purely by virtue of your accumulative Karma, both in this and many previous lives. You have already put in a great deal of work over many incarnations to come across this teaching, for by the law of Karma nothing happens by accident.

The wise person will accumulate skilful Karma and by so doing; will reduce the bank account of negative Karma.

If humanity could only realise the law of Karma, the world would be changed dramatically over night for the better.

We are letting our children down by not offering up this knowledge. If Karmic law was taught at an early age I am sure it would not be long before crime rates took a dramatic drop. Even if you do not subscribe to the law of Karma, ask yourself this question, ok, it can't be proven as in 'Look! Here is a bag of Karma,' but! What if? For in the same manner it can't be disproved, ask yourself, "What if I am wrong", surely it would be best to ere on the side of caution and go along with it, nothing to lose, but plenty to gain? Karma and reincarnation is an absolute given in many cultures, including ancient Egypt. Even the secret teachings of Judaism and Christianity subscribe to these two laws and is called Gilgal. The refutation and rejection of these two laws has caused much harm to not only humanity, but to the world in general.

Letting our children down? It is irresponsible to not relate the teaching of karma to our children. Worse still is to withhold the spiritual wisdom teachings of the world.

If you encounter difficulty and adversity, pain and suffering, internally give a quiet, humble thank you to the Divine for allowing you to pay that part of your Karma off. It is a little less to pay off and another step toward your final liberation. For every step you take towards God, towards the Divine – God, the Divine, will take one hundred towards you.

They who find the teaching of Karma unpalatable are those, generally, who are involved in wrongdoing, wrongdoing in this incarnation.

The law of Karma is exact; generally, there is no petition, we can ask and beg forgiveness as much as we like from the Divine. What we sow, so shall we reap.

A gangland figure in his last few days is lying on his hospital bed with his family gathered around; quietly he considers his life of crime and violence. He can't stop his thoughts about the pain and suffering he has wreaked upon many, many of whom must have had families just like him. Yet here, gathered before him, were his sons who would be taking over his empire of crime and violence. "Oh my God what have I done", he thought, but hang on a minute, why am I saying oh my God, I don't believe in God...but what if?...What really happens when you die?

There is also "collective Karma". This collective Karma best illustrates what we sow, so shall we reap, here is an example.

For many centuries now the human race has systematically raped and pillaged our mother earth of its natural resources. We breathe out carbon dioxide; trees breathe in carbon dioxide and breathe out oxygen; trees are the lungs of the planet.

Rain forests are being cut down at an alarming rate; the forests are needed for the exchange of gasses; hence pollution on the increase, air quality on the decrease.

Most of the Earth's natural resources will be depleted in a short space of time if this continues.

People in a position of power, who can influence what is happening to the earth, directly or otherwise, are in the process of creating terrible unskilful Karma.

The people responsible for the earth's demise will be directly reincarnated into the very worse areas of the planet earth.

As the human body sends out antibodies to destroy an attacking virus in order to maintain the body's balance and harmony, so it is with Mother Nature. She will destroy the virulent virus of the human race in order to maintain her balance and harmony. Human indifference is far more devastating than the weapons of mass destruction that we fear now, for the human race will make the whole planet *extinct* through its own lethargy.

War is wrong, no matter how we look at it. In the name of our country and earthly rulers, it is wrong. Worse still are wars in the name of God. God would never have us kill any of his creatures, let alone another human being.

God gave us free will; it is human beings that make war, not God, many of us blame God for our woes, but the truth is that the law of Karma is automatic; it has no Divine being making judgements. It is like flowers in spring-time, God does not have to intervene or persuade the flowers to come out of hibernation from the winter.

All of us have heard of air disasters were all passengers and crew have been killed with the exception of one or two people, it's seen as a miracle, Divine intervention, it may seem this way but it's not, it's simply the law of Karma.

Going to a far deeper level, even our thoughts create Karma, all you see before you started as a thought. The house you live in started as a thought, the chair; cooking utensils; ships; aircraft etc. Guard your thoughts, as you think today, so shall you be tomorrow. I am fed up, depressed; I am happy and blessed. Thoughts are your choice.

Positive Karma will aid in your ascent, negative Karma will move you to a descent, this, as you will see in a later chapter, is part of the symbolism of the Great Pyramid's ascending/descending passages.

So to you we say, continue to bank the skilful and positive Karma, thus moving ever onward and upward.

Try to remember you are not the body, you are not the mind, you are not the intellect, you are a being of light, a spiritual being, eternal and immortal, never born, never dyeing; only the body dies.

As more and more people awaken to this truth, then ever quicker will the golden age, an age of peace, harmony, joy and bliss, come into being. The golden age has to be brought in by humanity and humanity can only do this by raising its consciousness; the realisation it is inseparable from the Divine and each other.

All of humanity is partaking in creation via the manifestation of thoughts, the truth of thoughts manifesting has been well documented in Rhonda Byrne's "The Secret", although the author does miss an extremely important point in dealing with manifesting your heart's desire, Karma and intent.

Sadly, at present, collectively there is too much emphasis on negativity; we need to become more positive and optimistic. The human race needs to change its way of thinking.

Wisdom note:

'The watch you have may break some day or the other. But *this watch* is unbreakable - Watch whether you are speaking good or bad. Watch whether you abuse others or appreciate them.'

'You should not use your tongue to abuse others; abusing others is a sin. You cannot escape the consequences of your sinful acts. Everything has reaction, reflection and resound and it comes back to you in some form or the other. Hence, exercise control over the tongue...That is why it is said, *silence is golden*. Once words become less, the activities and vagaries of the mind also become less...Every sacred act has a manifold reward.' Sai Baba

The last and most important word on Karma, the pivotal point of Karma is intent. If your actions are premeditated, you intend an action; Karma will be created, positive or negative. If there is no intent the Karma is neutral.

By the law of Karma you have come across this teaching, as nothing happens by accident. Although your Karma has brought you here, I wish to emphasize that you have free will, you can step off the path at any time, but your efforts will not have been in vain. If and when you reincarnate, that which you have accomplished in this life will be with you.

Silt and Slime

What does the silt and slime constitute? Primarily it constitutes our conditioning; not only our parenting; also, our social environment; our belief systems (or non-belief), along with all that has gone before in previous incarnations.

Over many, many incarnations we have all built layer after layer of illusion, delusion and ignorance. It takes a huge effort, commitment, determination, courage and FOCUS to unravel all this conditioning.

All of us are to various degrees resistant to change; it takes the most open of minds to accept the possibility that we *could be wrong* in our perception of life and living. It takes great courage to begin to break down what we believe to be ourselves, that which fortifies the sense of "I", "ME" and "MINE." It takes even greater courage to continue this unravelling.

The greatest barrier to our realisation of Divinity is the EGO; we will focus in more detail on the ego shortly. Most importantly, we must first of all want change. If we are dissatisfied with who or what we have become, dissatisfied with our world; then change it. I*f you want something to change in your life; then change something in your life*.

At the end of this the darkest of Ages (the Kali Yuga), we have to contend with the influence of subtle persuasion. This actually creates further silt and slime so to speak. I am not saying all forms of media marketing; I am talking about that which fuels desire, greed, lust, and covetousness and campaigns that distort the truth. That which fuelled our original incarnation was a powerful desire to experience this creation. It is only by reversing this lust for the world that we can break this cycle of birth and rebirth. The key to breaking this hold is by nurturing a very powerful desire to return home.

We all need to question and ponder upon what is influencing our behaviour patterns and rise above this form of brain washing. We need to apply our intelligence; we need to ask ourselves, who is really benefiting by this subtle persuasion? Do I/we really need this or that? How many of us sit hour after hour in front of a television in a trance, being influenced in one way or another while the world passes us by. The subconscious mind if bombarded enough with information will be influenced.

Our conscious mind acts as a goal keeper to filter what we consider as acceptable. But the conscious mind will be unable to stop a continued onslaught, so that eventually, without us being aware, we will be influenced. Continuous awareness of the various sense stimuli strengthens the conscious mind, the goalkeeper.

Yes, it could be argued that what is written here is a form of brain washing, but it is not. As you read and carefully consider what is written here, you have the choice of taking this on board. All external stimuli which is continually bombarding the mind through varying types of media, doesn't really give you that choice.

This general awareness in Buddhism and Raja Yoga, is called "Mindfulness", however, this mindfulness extends to every aspect of life. A way of working on and perfecting our internal world is through watching our negative thought constructs. If you find yourself casting judgement on others, ask yourself, do I ever display those qualities? The prophet Moses was mighty in word and deed – consider your thoughts, words and deeds, are they compassionate and caring? Or do they cause division, confrontation and strife?

So, there is external silt and slime, and there is internal silt and slime. There is our pre-conditioning, that which we bring with us into the world (internal), and that which continues to condition via environmental influence (external).

This carrying over of traits from one life to another is what shapes our interests, our focus and our direction. It is not always the case that an unruly child is the product of bad parenting, the history of the incarnating soul is a major factor. In short, our destiny is being written by our own hands in this and any subsequent incarnations.

To live by a moral code, to live a virtuous life, will go a long way in lifting us out of the silt and slime; to socialize with like-minded people, spiritual and wise. To discriminate as in "deserve/doesn't deserve", will help us greatly.

That which finally washes away the silt and slime, and purifies us, is our spiritual practice (Sadhana), immersing ourselves in the waters of the Divine. There are five important keys to ascension: Prayer; Mantra; Meditation; Focus; Affirmation and Aspiration.

CHAPTER 13

KEY COMPONENTS

Focus

Just like the Lotus flower with its mission to reach up to the light, so it is with the aspiring spiritual student. The spiritual student has one mission in life, and that is to re-unite with God, with the Divine, with the light of God.

Somewhat puzzling is the belief of the western New Age concept of what it is to be spiritual as opposed to religious. I know so many people who embrace this New Age concept. If you reject religion and embrace such subjects as Tarot, Runes, Magic, Astrology, to name but a few, it is seen that you are spiritual. For most it becomes nothing more than an intellectual exercise. The focus has become distorted and has no real affirmation or "aspiration", essential to an active transformational process.

Keeping the mind focused on the Divine is very important, for as the spiritual student continues to aspire, the student becomes ever riper; the petals of the lotus flower slowly begin to open.

Imagine yourself to be an Archer, drawing back the arrow, firmly fixing your focus on the centre of the target, become one with the bow, the arrow, the target...the target is God, be one with God, you are any way.

Personally, I use a number of tools to keep focused on the Divine. I know exactly what the Great Pyramid represents. Whenever my eyes set upon an image of this pyramid, I immediately think of God. So, living in a country that has a lot of rain fall most buildings have gabled roofs; prominent gables that resemble the pyramid brings my focus back on the Divine. In the city where I live we have a multitude of religious festivals, so whenever there is a festival, Muslim, Christian, Sikh, Hindu etc. my mind refocuses on the Divine. The same thing happens whenever seeing a Mosque, a church, a temple. Where I work there are so many diverse faiths, whenever I see an image of the Divine: the symbol of Islam, the Christian Cross, Hindu Deities, Sikh pictures of Guru Nanak, pictures of the Buddha etc. I give an internal salutation.

Fundamentally, use anything that is useful in bringing the mind back to the Divine. Another tool I use in everyday life connects the heart to God which is very important – music. When listening to music on the radio, say when driving, I sing along with the song, but change the lyrics in appropriate places, thus singing about my love for God; a rather difficult task with Gangster Rap! I also play my favourite devotional and aspirational music as I go to sleep. My favourite artist is Kate Bush and I especially love her album *Hounds of Love.*

Aspiration

Aspiration is doing, to be persistent in your search, in your practice. Aspire to reach and even surpass the heights of the spiritual greats, the Buddha, Shivpuri Baba etc. If they can do it, so can you. Aspire to re-unite with God, with the Divine – make this your mission in life.

It states in the Bible that "When Moses hands were raised, he was assured of victory". The hand in esoteric Judaism is used as a metaphor for the spirit – so for as long as his spirits were raised/confident, he would attain his goal...endeavour to keep your hands raised through difficult times.

Just a word of advice here, do not let your search bog you down with too many books, by all means research as I did, but eventually decide *to do*, have a balance. The mind and the intellect have a ceiling. A classic example of unnecessary fluctuation I have witnessed, is spiritual aspirants finally being drawn to an Avatar. Their devotion is wonderful, but suddenly out of the blue they say, 'Oh, I have just finished reading...he's amazing, you should read it.' The book is from an ordinary human being who is aspiring and yes, can be amazing and inspirational. There is absolutely nothing wrong with reading spiritually focused books – but watch your mind. Ask yourself, am I grabbing book after book to avoid actually walking the path?

That which comes from an Avatar is very different – find an Avatar's teaching and stick with it...aspire to meld with the Avatar.

So to aspire, as in Moses edict, is to want God, to want God with all your heart, with your entire mind, with all your soul and with all your strength.

THE FINAL GREAT PATH

Affirmation

Affirmation is also very important, continue to affirm that you are one with the Divine, you are one with God. Affirm that you are a spiritual being on a material journey, that your body is your vehicle to experience this material realm. Your body is the host of the real you...not the ego.

Affirm that the truth is, that you were never born and never will you die, the body may die but you are not the body.

Sadly, humanity has forgotten the reason for incarnating; the mission for humanity is remember the Divine and to become realized. Your real mission in this life is to *aspire* to the truth. As Jesus said: *The truth will set you free.*

Being mindful, when you notice negative or frivolous thoughts whirring around your mind, bring them to a halt and repeat inwardly, *I am one with God, one with the Divine*, over and over again.

See the whole of creation as Sahaja, as just one Divine energy expressing itself in a multitude of forms. See everything as atoms just vibrating at a different rate. Acknowledging this scientific truth, that all is atoms, all is one singular Divine energy, including your body, is to affirm you are inseparable and one with the Divine and the whole of creation.

Prayer

Prayer is very powerful as it connects us directly to God. Pray for world peace, pray for help with your Divine quest and ask God to reveal ever more to you.

If you have never prayed before, it will seem strange at first, it will feel as if you are talking to yourself, but in a spiritually profound manner you will be.

You will be talking to the supreme, the nature of prayer is to ask over and over again for the same thing, as opposed to just chit chat. However, the latter is also a good practice to just chit chat to the Divine (but be careful there's no-one around when you do, otherwise you could be carried off in a straight-jacket), by doing so you are immersing yourself in the Divine.

`Please Lord elevate humanity's consciousness to such a level that there is no more need for our negative ego attributes. Please help me over my difficulties. Please help my friend who is not very well. Please help me to become ever stronger in my desire to be one with you again. Please help me to become ego-less, to drop the "I". Please bring about world peace as soon as possible and above all; please don't let them lock me up for being mad.`

Offer everything you do to God, all you eat and drink; by doing this all becomes sanctified, blessed and holy. Food and drink that is offered up to God becomes blessed and is known as Prasad, but whenever we do not offer up food or drink to the Divine, in effect it is stolen.

All your work, all your activities, offer them up to God, to the Divine, this is the "very quickest way" to reunion with God, with the Divine.

If you notice the mind has wandered into frivolous or negative thoughts, repeat a Mantra (a selection of Mantras will be given), or just repeat the name of your God or chosen Deity. This following true story ties in the reality of both prayer and Karma:

My uncle Monty (a devout Roman Catholic), was staying at a hotel. In the night he got up to go to the bathroom, but he was sleep walking. Taking his usual turn he would have taken at home, he went down the stairs. My uncle, unconscious, was whisked off to hospital in a critical condition. He was taken into intensive care where he lay in a coma; the prognosis was bleak.

A series of dedicated Masses for him were held at the church, along with a request for the whole congregation to pray for his recovery. Six weeks later he had made a miraculous full recovery, could this have been Divine intervention – prayers being answered? Maybe, maybe not.

Six months later, my uncle and auntie were over in Ireland visiting an old friend. During the night he got up to go to the bathroom, but he was sleep walking again; down the stairs he went, only this time...he was dead.

Karma is Karma, he was meant to go in this manner, but the fervent prayers from the congregation had delivered a respite for those who loved my uncle, and yet only delayed the inevitable karmic outcome.

Wisdom note:

'Divinity is the same in everyone, be he/she a Hindu, a Muslim, a Sikh or a Christian. There is only one religion, the religion of love. There is only one caste, the caste of humanity. So develop unity, chant the Divine Name. What an exalted position will the country attain if all its people were to chant the Divine Name together!...One who cultivates the crop of love in the field of one's heart is a true Christian, a true Sikh, a true Hindu and a true Muslim etc.' Sai Baba

THE FINAL GREAT PATH

Mantra

Mantra, for want of a better description, is the science of sound. All sounds have a vibration; all sounds will have an effect upon us in one way or another.

If you were approached by a person, who then told you they hated you, this would provoke a negative response of thought, feeling and possibly action. And yet, if that same person told you they loved you, the result would be totally different.

The above explanation is extremely simplistic. We could keep repeating Fish, Chips & Mushy Peas all we like, the only thing we would accomplish would probably be a trip to the local Fish and Chip shop.

Mantra is divinely inspired and like prayer connects us directly to the Divine; its vibration is such that it affects us on a much more profound level, it even has the power to actually change molecular structure within the body.

Mantra will also have a positive effect on how we feel; whenever negative thoughts enter the mind, repeat a Mantra, in this way there is no room for negative thoughts to enter.

Although the following examples of Mantra are from Sanskrit records, it should not be assumed that they belong to any one particular religion.

All true Mantras should just be seen as from God, as from the Divine.

If you feel uncomfortable with any of the following Mantras, just repeat the name of your chosen Deity.

Selection of Mantras:

OM NAMO SHIVAYA (I am one with God)
OM SRI SATYA SAI KRISNAI NAMAHA
OM NAMO BAGAVATA MATER MEERA
OM MUNI PADMAY HUM
OM PIREETA (healing Mantra)
OM NAMO BAGAVATA AVATAR HARI KRISHNA. HARI is pronounced with a soft "A" as in car; its meaning is, "He who takes away"
SO-HAM – before meditating; breathing in and out through the nose, on the in-breath mentally say "So", on the out-breath "Ham", So-Ham means "I am He" Half a minute should be ample

These do not have to be vocalized (although it is quite nice to get a real resonance going), you can do Mantra mentally. If you do not like the above you may just wish to do something like the following. "God, God, Allah, Allah, God, God, Allah, Allah", etc. Or, "God, God, Jesus, Jesus", etc.

As previously mentioned, as we bring all of these elements together, just like a radio we begin to tune into the Divine – once tuned in we activate resonant frequency becoming one with the Divine.

Wisdom note:

'Develop steadiness in the recitation of the Name of God and in the worth of that Name. Then, even if the whole world says, "Do evil", you will refuse to obey; your system itself will revolt against it. And even if the whole world asks you to desist, you will insist on doing the right. You have to cultivate four types of strength: Strength of body, intellect, wisdom and conduct. Then you become unshakable; you are on the path of spiritual victory.' Sai Baba

CHAPTER 14

MEDITATION

Meditation has been around for thousands of years. In ancient India (once known as Mahabharata), it was and still is used by men and women aspiring to fathom the truth of our existence, these people were, and still are to this day known as Yogis. The word Yoga has a double meaning; in the first instance yoga means to unite, to join. So in the context of these yogis they were/are aspiring to unite with their Divine origin. In the second instance it means to yoke as in the context of carrying a burden; the burden being everything that binds us to the material world. So in this context the Yogi is trying to disengage from that which entraps.

In ancient Egypt meditation was part of daily life, although eventually it was withheld from the masses and became exclusive to royalty, the priests and those who served in the temples. The same happened in India when it became exclusive to the Brahmins. The exception to this rule was a small minority who broke away from their would-be masters, taking the sacred knowledge underground.

In the east this took the form of Holy Sages and isolated Gurus (teachers). In the west the sacred knowledge took the form of hidden or esoteric lore, guarded by select groups such as The Knights Templar and certain monastic orders.

The esoteric orders of the west also developed an outer order and an inner order, and even within the inner order or court, there developed a further inner order, so the teachings became ever more exclusive and remote.

This same pattern continued around the world throughout all cultures, from Druids through to Shamans, from Shamans to Fakirs and Medicine men, but what was the reason behind this? It was the same throughout the world then as it is today. In the first instance the secular precept is "*Keep the people ignorant and you hold the corridors of power...knowledge is power*". In the second instance, that of the west, the custodians of this sacred knowledge had to go underground for self-preservation and to protect this knowledge from secularism and the profane.

To aspire to spiritual truth is to unite with your original nature; your original nature is that of a peaceful harmonious being, a spiritual being of light.

This knowledge is the birth right of the whole of humanity and when all of humanity realizes this truth, peace will reign and humanity will begin to break its chains of self-imposed bondage.

In the meantime, you can make a difference, for as you become more spiritual a vibration of peace, harmony and calmness will begin to emanate from you. Your candle of light will have been lit; you can then gently light the candles of those who will seek you out.

Today this knowledge is being given to you freely, without hidden agenda, the chance and opportunity of freedom. What exactly then is this freedom? It is arriving at the truth that you are in this world but not of it; it brings a sense of relief; in as much that you no longer have to keep up with the Jones's of this world. You will no longer feel compelled to compete, for the only adversary is yourself, your own ego.

So, what exactly is meditation? It is a method of placing the body in a very stable posture (asana) that allows the practitioner to feel safe and confident.

A stable posture ensures stability, so when honing and focusing the mind on other than the body, the body will not fall over. The posture will also allow the free flow of energy around the body, all without the need to think about it.

In its most basic form, meditation can be used for stress relief and relaxation; it has many benefits upon the health of the regular practitioner.

For most people in this current age, life is extremely hectic, so much so that the mind is continually racing around, even when retiring to go to bed; the mind is still whirring around.

The human brain can operate on five different frequencies: Alpha, Beta, Delta, Theta and Gamma. For most of humanity the brain resonates at the beta frequency. When meditating, the brain in due course changes frequency.

1. Beta (14-40Hz) — the waking consciousness and reasoning wave

Beta brain waves are associated with normal waking consciousness and a heightened state of alertness, logic and critical reasoning. While Beta brain waves are important for effective functioning throughout the day, they can also translate into stress, anxiety and restlessness. The voice of Beta can be described as being that nagging little inner critic that gets louder with five sense bombardment.

Therefore, with a majority of adults operating at Beta; its little surprise that stress is today's most common health problem.

2. Alpha (7.5-14Hz) — the deep relaxation wave

Alpha brain waves are present in deep relaxation and usually when the eyes are closed, when you're slipping into a lovely daydream or during light meditation. It is an optimal time to program the mind for success and it also heightens your imagination, visualization, memory, learning and concentration. It is the gateway to your subconscious mind and lies at the base of your conscious awareness. The voice of Alpha is your intuition, which becomes clearer and more profound the closer you get to 7.5Hz.

3. Theta (4-7.5Hz) — the deep meditation and sleeping wave

Theta brain waves are present during deep meditation and light sleep, including the all-important REM dream state. It is the realm of your sub consciousness and only experienced momentarily as you drift off to sleep from Alpha and wake from deep sleep from Delta. It is said that a sense of deep spiritual connection and unity with the universe can be experienced at Theta. Your mind's most deep-seated programs are at Theta and it is where you experience vivid visualizations, great inspiration, profound creativity and exceptional insight. Unlike your other brain waves, the elusive voice of Theta is a silent voice.

It is at the Alpha-Theta border, from 7Hz to 8Hz, where the optimal range for visualization, mind programming and using the creative power of your mind begins. It's the mental state which you consciously create your reality. At this frequency, you are conscious of your surroundings, however your body is in deep relaxation.

4. Delta (0.5-4Hz) — the deep sleep wave

The Delta frequency is the slowest of the frequencies and is experienced in deep, dreamless sleep and in very deep, transcendental meditation where awareness is fully detached. Delta is the realm of your unconscious mind, and the gateway to the universal mind and the collective unconscious, where information received is otherwise unavailable at the conscious level. Among many things, deep sleep is important for the healing process — as it's linked with deep healing and regeneration. Hence, not having enough deep sleep is detrimental to your health in more ways than one.

5. Gamma (above 40Hz) – The Insight Wave

This range is the most recently discovered and is the fastest frequency at above 40Hz. While little is known about this state of mind, initial research shows Gamma waves are associated with bursts of insight and high-level information processing

Meditation is a method of regaining control of the mind, of calming the thought process down, which leads on to a very relaxed state of consciousness, and a place of peace that lies within the consciousness of the practitioner.

With steady practice, it will produce a steady and calm approach to life, concentration and focus will be enhanced dramatically, tasks that seemed to be very difficult and stressful become markedly so much easier.

On a higher level, i.e. on a spiritual footing, meditation is a method and means to facilitate a rising in consciousness of our Divine origin, of our true Divine identity, which is known as self-realization; it is a method for connecting to our Divine source which is God.

This is done by gaining complete control over the mind in every aspect, i.e. the thought and reasoning faculty, along with the emotional faculty, while at the same time, losing body consciousness. For the spiritual practitioner a belief and faith in the Divine is essential.

Your body posture is very important and is known as an asana, loose and comfy clothing is essential. The following are quite common postures used for the purpose of meditation, but this list is by no means definitive.

Egyptian Asana

This is done by sitting on a chair (see fig. 1); an ordinary dining chair is ideal. It may help to place a length of wood approximately two to three inches thick under the rear legs of your chair. This throws your weight forward onto your feet and accommodates the natural angle of the pelvis. Make sure that the chair is stable; the last thing you would want is for you and the chair to topple over halfway through your meditation – not conducive to peace and bliss.

Fig. 1: Egyptian Posture

Having removed shoes and socks, sit on the edge of the chair, your heels touching, this forms what is known as a Prana lock (Prana means vital energy, known as Chi in China, and Ki in Japan and Korea). Your hands will now form a mudra (mudra means formal hand position). There are quite a number of different mudras; here we will give you a choice of two.

Touch the forefinger and thumb together to form a circle (see fig. 2), extend the remaining fingers out, the three extended fingers held together. Place the hands onto the thighs palms down, or palms up, whichever is the most comfortable. This forms a second Prana lock. Prana locks are important in as much as they hold this vital energy within the body, preventing its dispersal back to the earth. This particular Mudra allows excess Prana/Chi to exit the three fingers, either back up to the heavens (palm up), or back to the earth (palm down).

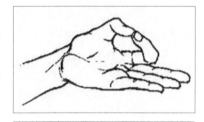

Fig. 2

The spine should be straight; shoulders slightly back; chin slightly tucked in; this will keep straight the cervical (neck) vertebrae. Your buttocks should feel as if they are pushing down to earth, your head should feel as if it is pushing up to heaven. Now place the tip of the tongue on your upper hard pallet just behind the front teeth (by pronouncing the word/name EL, the tongue finds its proper place), this forms a third and final Prana lock. All this comes together to form your Egyptian asana.

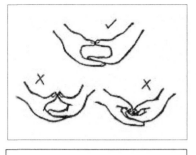

Fig. 3

An alternate mudra: Place the left hand into the right hand (see fig. 3); now touch the tip of the thumbs together. The thumbs should run parallel with the floor; the hands held approximately two inches below the navel (although not critical) also parallel to the floor.

Mountain Asana

This is done by kneeling (see fig. 4), the left big toe crosses over the right big toe (Prana lock), adopt the mudra of your choice, then apply the above instructions of the Egyptian posture i.e. straight back and neck, tongue position etc.

A stool can be made (recommended), to make kneeling dramatically easier.

Fig. 4

To make this, attach two supports either end of a piece of wood that is approximately eighteen inches long and approximately eight inches wide. Each support should be approximately eight inches in length at the back and six and a half inches at the front. This will tilt the supports natural to the pelvis angle, making sitting more comfortable. These may be attached using hinges, so that the supports will fold in for easy transportation.

This posture is also sometimes referred to as the Vajra (Thunderbolt), posture or Za-Zen posture. It is tempting to suggest that the kneeling position adopted in Christian Churches was originally the Mountain posture, but over many hundreds of years, its purpose became lost, and is now interpreted as a position of penitence and servility.

Half Lotus or Perfect Posture

Sitting on the floor tuck your left heel under the groin. Next place your right instep onto your left thigh. Apply the same format as the Egyptian asana i.e. straight back, Prana/Chi locks etc. You may find it helpful to make one or two cushions (see fig.5), to sit on; very dense foam is ideal. Each cushion should be approximately 12 inches in diameter, and approximately 4 - 6 inches in depth; covers may be made to preserve the dense foam.

Fig.5

This posture, unless the practitioner is very supple, is extremely difficult to do, and can be very uncomfortable, which of course would defeat the objective of total relaxation; it is better to adopt a posture that best suits you.

The Corpse Posture

This is done by lying down on the floor or on your bed, arms relaxed down by your sides, either palms up or down, the key is to be comfortable and relaxed, the same criteria apply of back and neck straight, tongue position etc.

The only drawback with this posture is that it is very easy to end up falling asleep, this should be avoided. It is very important to hold the concentration and awareness, if you allow yourself to keep falling asleep it will become a habit that is difficult to break. If at any time you feel you may be nodding off to sleep, it is better to terminate that particular session, this is true for all meditation.

A formal meditation posture is assumed for a number of reasons:

1. To place the body in a comfortable but stable position, so as not to be worried about your body's safety

2. To allow an unimpaired flow of energy around the body

3. To keep erect the spine in alignment with the cervical vertebrae, so allowing the easy rising of what is known as the Kundalini. The Kundalini is a spiritual energy that lays dormant at the base of the spine in all human beings; this subject will be covered a little latter

Wisdom note:

'A real vision brings adoration of the Divine and in that adoration there can be no vanity. Real visions are helpful and bring positive change, but be careful as the mind can be deceptive. Some will have visions, some not; real visions deepen faith, they show you what you should aim for – be grateful for these but don't make the acquisitions of visions your goal.

The real work is in building love and silence; in changing your whole character and mind, visions come and go but the silence remains. The silence brings continual connection, continual Divine presence.' Mother Meera.

There is a multitude of types and ways to meditate; ranging from various forms of visualization, to concentrating on external objects, to concentrating on breathing. Here we will give you only those totally safe to do. The vast majority of those not mentioned here, require a teacher.

Meditative Practice – Vapasna

The two basic forms of Vapasna concentrate on the breath:

1. Sitting in the asana of your choice, breath in and out through the nose, if for medical reasons this cannot be done then breath through the mouth.

With eyes closed focus the mind at a point approximately two inches below the navel and approximately two inches within. Breathe naturally from the stomach as opposed to the upper chest. Try to empty the mind of all thoughts as you do this.

A very helpful tool in controlling the mind is to count the breaths, each time you conclude the breath in, count one – pause for a second or two, conclude breath out count two and pause, breath in count three, breath out count four, all the way up to ten, and then start at one again. If you find the mind wanders, just gently bring it back to your practice, do not get annoyed if this happens and just smile inwardly thanking the Divine for the test. It is important to have a light, joyful attitude to your practice, enjoy

2.   With eyes closed focus the mind just below the tip of the nose. Feel the quality of breath on the tip; is it warm or cold, moist or dry?

Alternatively, focus just below the tip of the nose. On the in breath, just as the inhalation comes to its completion, count one and pause, breath out and pause, breath in, count two, breath out, breath in count three etc. all the way up to ten, pausing at each in and out breath, then restart at one again. You've probably noticed that in the first practice you count on both inhaling and exhaling, whereas in this practice it's only on the in-breath. The first practice ties the mind down more than the second, it gives the mind less space in which to wander; you can employ either counting method.

Alternatively repeat in your mind, "Ha" (as in car), on completing the in breath: Ha = God within and "Ka" (again as in car) on completing the out breath; God without

The mind will do its best to prevent you from controlling it, the mind has been allowed a free reign for a very long time and will wish for that to continue.

Practice once or twice a day. Two or three minutes each time to start with will be ample. This can be gradually increased as you gain proficiency, but always remember it is the quality rather than the quantity that counts.

Try to set a specific time of day to do this, getting up a little earlier is a very good idea, this way the mind cannot fool you into making the excuse of "I don't have the time".

Avoid the temptation to keep chopping and changing your meditation, choose one after trying each one out, then stick with it for three months. If after three months you feel you would like to change, then fine, do so. Be aware that the mind will find excuses for you to discontinue this practice, it is very clever, and will come up with excuses such as "I can't get on with this; I can't get comfy; I will never get to grips with my mind".

Similarly, you will find in the early stages that the mind has the power to create itches, and irritations all over the body, usually starting with itches to the face, try to ignore these, eventually they do stop. Then the mind will play other tricks, such as hone in and focus on external noises, saying to you, 'How on earth can I meditate with this noise going on,' again it's just a trick of the mind, that once you have pushed through, will give you powers of tremendous concentration.

Another very common occurrence with meditation is that of salivating. The mouth fills with saliva, this is perfectly normal, in time this also becomes less and less frequent and will eventually stop. You have two choices, either swallow, or dribble.

The important thing is to enjoy this relaxing activity, don't get frustrated, some sessions will go very well, some not so well, it is all part of the mind game.

If at all possible, try to face east; this relates to the energy fields that run throughout the planet.

As the final great path is one of fixing the heart and mind on God/the Divine, once settled for meditation, say a little prayer to God, Avatar or chosen Deity. Ask to be opened ever more to the Divine light and if at all appropriate, to allow you to experience the Divine presence.

If you suddenly find yourself levitating, don't worry, they don't charge airport tax, as yet, for levitating bodies.

Wisdom note:

'We have to recognize that human life depends on the functioning of the mind. As long as one is governed by the mind, one continues to be human. Once one goes beyond the mind, one can enjoy the vastness of the limitless expanse of Cosmic Consciousness. Here is an example: Suppose you construct a spacious house with a number of bedrooms, living rooms, dining room and bath room. The house appears divided into a number of small rooms. This is because of the walls put up for partitioning into rooms. If the walls are pulled down, the house will be one vast mansion. Similarly, the body is the wall which limits one's perception to the narrow confines of the body. Once you get rid of this body consciousness, you will experience the vast expanse of the Universal Cosmic Consciousness which is all-pervasive.' Sai Baba

CHAPTER 15

CONNECTING

The effect of combining all of the foregoing is to gradually increase the amount of time you focus upon the Divine.

If you imagine your usual day as a pie chart, try to devote one segment to the Divine. There is no hard and fast rule or law as to how much time, the important point is, devote some of it.

We do not have to go to a place of worship to do this, humanity built places of worship, not God.

This is not to say that places of worship are without value, quite the opposite in fact, for places of worship set up a unique vibration. Places of worship are a place to meet like-minded people, friendship with spiritually focused people will aid in ascension.

It is also helpful to our aspiration to visit holy places, places of all types of religion; we should always respect other faiths and religions as *the final great path has no room for extremists.*

As we proceed with our practice, we slowly find that the segment in our pie chart grows.

The Ideal is to nurture a continual connection with the Divine; this can even be carried over into your sleeping state. When getting tucked up in bed, lay there for a few minutes, ask God to help you to carry your practice over into the sleeping state, ask God to visit you in your dreams, lay there doing Mantra (heartfelt) until dropping off to sleep.

With respect to dreams, most dreams are of no significance what-so-ever, it is the subconscious mind ridding itself of superfluous material, a bit like emptying the recycle bin of a computer. Dreams that have an Avatar in them, such as Sai Baba, Mother Meera, Jesus or Krishna are indeed meaningful, the recipient is being graced. A Divine dream promotes love, peace and harmony, if the dream doesn't promote these qualities it can be ignored.

Free will

We must keep reinforcing this fact. You have free will, at any point you decide to change your focus you are quite within your rights. Here I would just like to take this opportunity to go into free will a little deeper.

As the apparent separation took place from God so as to incarnate into the material world, it was agreed that we would have free will. We were adamant that we would not forget our Divine origin...but we did. God agreed to free will through his love for his children, but having agreed, he promised he would never go back on his word. The law of Karma was put in place, which again was agreed and made irreversible along with reincarnation. Reincarnation exists in order to re-balance our impact upon this earthly plain.

To escape reincarnation and return to God, the material world can be likened to a sort of giant maze. Most of humanity wander around this maze aimlessly; acquiring stores of all manner of goods, things that can't be taken with you, far better is to search out the knowledge of God, and how to return.

For those who begin to search for a way out, for a way back to God, clues start to appear, clues that will point us in the right direction. The ultimate clue in this giant maze and reminder as to "the way" back home, other than Avatars, is the Great Pyramid of Gizeh.

The ills of this world are a direct result of misuse of free will. As soon as humanity aligns the heart and mind with the Divine, then and only then will the ills of this world be healed.

It is pointless, although understandable why people say, 'How can God allow this to happen, there can't be a God for otherwise God would intervene.'

The above explains why God does not intervene, but *we can*. We have free will to wander around the maze of the material world aimlessly, but it is a cold wind blowing if this is what we choose to do. Or we can also exercise free will, and look for a way out of this maze by turning to the warmth and sunshine of God, of the Divine. And as we go on our way, spread the message of love, peace and harmony through our thoughts words and deeds.

THE FINAL GREAT PATH

The cup overflows

So far, we have been striving to a greater degree on the internal, on the Body/Mind/Spirit.

As soon as we feel comfortable with this re-alignment so to speak, we can then turn our attention outwardly again.

Ancient and current Masters refer to the external world, the sensual world, as Maya, Maya means illusion. All seems so real from a human perspective, for after all when we bang our toe on a denser structure, it hurts.

From a human perspective, living in a body of form, we perceive the material world via the five senses, that of sight, sound, touch, taste and smell.

Science has long known that everything is made up of Atoms, particles that vibrate at differing frequencies. All around us is made up of the same material, even going out to the Sun, the Moon and Stars; all is made up of Atoms vibrating at different rates, but Atoms all the same.

Even gasses comprise of atoms, the air we breathe comprises of atoms. As air is not a solid and fills the spaces between all material forms, it gives the impression of duality and multiplicity.

Science understands the world as made up of atoms, so therefore the body is made up of atoms.

All *is* the Divine, there is no duality or separation...multiplicity is illusion. Eventually we begin to perceive that all is Maya, all is illusion; we begin to perceive that all around us and within us is one mass of Divine energy. The Divine has allowed just a miniscule part of itself to vibrate at a much slower rate to create the illusion of the world of time, space and form.

To help your understanding; sea water evaporates to begin a new journey and forms clouds, the clouds disperse as rain over mountain tops to form a river. Now imagine a massive river that suddenly cascades over a huge cliff forming a waterfall. As the water goes over the edge it breaks up into billions of water particles, all seemingly distinct and separate. But the moment the particles hit the bottom they re-merge to form the river again. This river makes its way to the great sea, where it once again becomes one with the sea. The human race is like the water going over the cliff as a waterfall; seemingly separate like the individual water particles...in human terms we are making our way back to the sea of God.

When we see all as the Divine, as God (known in Sanskrit as Sahaja), it becomes obvious why God is omnipotent and omniscient. Gradually we begin to see that if we cause harm; we will be harming ourselves as everything is one great unity. If you didn't exist, then nothing would exist.

Now we are no longer just internalizing our Sadhana, our spiritual practice, but by seeing the sensual world around us as a part of the Divine manifestation, our spiritual awareness is now overflowing outwardly. Our practice now becomes like breathing, breathing in and breathing out; the function of breathing itself can impart a spiritual lesson to us also.

Hidden within this unnoticed bodily function lays a code of spiritual conduct, for whenever we breathe in we are receiving oxygen, whenever we breathe out we give back carbon dioxide. In fact we are exchanging gifts with the trees as trees breath in carbon dioxide and breath out oxygen; in order to receive we should always give, it is cyclic in nature.

If all we do is taking, take, take, eventually all will be taken away. This is the law of Karma. If not taken away in this lifetime, it will be taken the next.

Appreciation is very, very important. Before eating and drinking, offer it up to the Divine or your chosen Deity and thank the living entity that gave its life for you where appropriate and pray it didn't suffer. If we do not make this offering, as mentioned, the food and drink is in effect, stolen.

Don't take anything for granted, whenever doing your shopping, thank the Divine for this incredible grace. When seeing extremely busy supermarkets and witness rudeness and aggression in many shoppers – it is difficult not to get upset at such behaviour. This may help, every single person in that superstore has earnt the amazing grace of such plenty spread before them. In previous lives they have helped the needy, sacrificed their own needs for others.

Of course, the problem is that none of us can recall these previous lives. The result is that over time we take it for granted and become complacent. So, what will be the outcome of such unacceptable behaviour and greed? In distant continents men, women and children are starving and bereft of clean drinking water – where then do you think we will be reincarnated in our next life?

Thank the Lord for the roof over your head, all amenities such as electricity, heat, water, the bathroom, the bed you sleep in and the pillow and covers that keep you warm. Basically everything, thank the Divine and offer it up. From time to time, when breathing, breathe in, breathe out and mentally say thank you. When swinging your legs out of bed in the morning, as soon as your feet touch the floor, give a thank you for being allowed to wake to the start of another day. When seeing an emergency first responder vehicle, ask God to bless the crew for the amazing job they do.

Wisdom note:

'What is required is a synthesis of both the inner and outer lives.' Sai Baba

Interaction with the outside world

It is very important that you continue to have what is considered to be a normal interaction with the world, do not seek to escape the world.

At one stage in my quest for truth, I considered an alternative life in an Ashram. I attended retreats to Buddhist ashrams and although this was of great value at the time, after much contemplation of this way of life I decided ashram life was not the way. The truth should be open to all, no matter what you may be doing, no matter where you may live.

Ashrams are fine, provided that they are used purely for educational reasons to be taught and study under a Master, three to five years for those with this inclination would be ample.

Once you have ascended the mountain, you should descend the mountain so others will have access to your knowledge. One word of caution, never try to force spirituality on anyone, people who are ready will naturally gravitate towards you.

To have the light of spiritual knowledge poured in, and then only to remain in an Ashram would be a selfish act; what would be the point of hiding a beacon under a bucket?

Enjoy your life as a human, be light hearted and joyous, enjoy normal human activity.

Do not become stern, do not become ascetic and start beating yourself, either physically, or metaphorically – have a smile.

Beware of looking for faults in others, this is an ego trait, become your own gardener and weed out your own faults.

If you notice negative traits in others, ask yourself if you also are like this or like that, weed out the undesired traits, thank Paramatman (the Supreme Being) for making you aware.

Wisdom note:

'To have spirituality is to love; aspire to; remember; surrender to the Divine; to have spirituality doesn't mean that one shouldn't have a full life in the world. One should not leave the world...but the Divine should come first.' Sai Baba

Duty

If you are single, and have no dependants, going to live in an ashram for a while would be acceptable. If married, if you have dependants, this would not be acceptable.

My teacher incarnated as an ordinary householder. He married, raised a family, went to work, and led an ordinary life. This was done to show humanity the way, he led by example.

First and foremost, you have a duty to your body, keeping it clean and healthy. Secondly you have a duty to your spouse and to your dependants.

Wherever possible you should work to pay your way in society. As we tread the final great path, it is essential to have a code of conduct.

For me, I have drawn strength from my martial arts, in Zenyogkido, which translates as the way of the mind, body and spirit; we have what is known as the 9 virtues of:

HUMANITY
HUMILITY
HONOR
KINDNESS
COURAGE
COURTESY
KNOWLEDGE
WISDOM
LOYALTY

In tandem with the nine virtues; the code of conduct we aspire to live by, we have the Three Gems, essential to progress along the final great path, these should not be confused with the Three Jewels of Buddhism:

RIGHT BELIEF – RIGHT KNOWLEDGE – RIGHT CONDUCT

Shrines

It is very nice to have a shrine/shrine room if your circumstances permit, although not essential. It is important to have somewhere to go and meditate knowing that you will not be disturbed.

Friends of mine, Peter and Debs, have a shrine set up in their spare bedroom; you can feel the power of Divine presence as soon as you come to the bedroom door.

Eventually realize that you can meditate almost anywhere, that the shrine/shrine room is a spiritual crutch to help you on your way.

If you decide that you can only practice your Sadhana at the shrine, you will be setting up a prison for yourself.

If you have a picture of an Avatar or chosen Deity, always give salutation, if not externally, then internally. The picture is far more than just a picture.

CHAPTER 16

THE EGO

The ego is a very slippery character; it was given to us at our very first incarnation, its function then was simply that of survival, fight or flight.

Over each successive incarnation, as our intelligence grew, so did our egos. The ego is everything we believe to be our identity as a separate self- contained individual, it's what we believe to be, `I`, `Me`, and `Mine`.

The ego is known in the western hidden teachings as, "the little i". The ego, is what we believe to be our real self, but in reality is not. It will do anything, and everything it can to prevent its decline.

In Ancient Egypt the ego was depicted as the God Typhon/Set. Typhon or Set represented the little "I". The God Horus, whom Set (brother of Horus), went to war with in a battle of sovereignty, represented our higher self the Atman, hence his ideographic form as a hawk or falcon headed God representing the transcendental greater "I".

Set was also represented as a Hippopotamus. This was to depict the sheer size and ugliness of the over inflated ego.

There are many anecdotes of the battles between Horus and Set (the higher and lower self), shown in the hieroglyphics of that period. The Hippopotamus shrinks in size during or after many of these battles, only to grow in size once again.

I mention the decreasing in size of the Hippopotamus here, as this is precisely what happens to the ego, over a period of time, with the persistence of our spiritual practice the ego shrinks. The ego will shrink, although it will never disappear completely as it will always have a function in the material world. The ego will always seek to grow in influence and dominance – a peace between the two needs to be sought. This reality was portrayed in the story of Typhon and Horus agreeing to a truce; depicted in Egyptian iconography as Sam-Tui. This

Sam-Tui is illustrated by the Gods Typhon/Set and Horus either side of a pole holding each end of a vine/rope that is attached to the pole, it symbolises joint sovereignty.

In dealing with the ego it is far better to adopt a gentle approach, 'Thank you for bringing me this far, but your service is no longer needed.'

Repeat to yourself many times, 'I am an actor playing the part of a butler, I have played this part for many, many incarnations. I have played it so well, I have begun to believe I am actually the butler, but my true reality is that I am a spiritual being, a being of light, eternal and immortal, never born and never dying.'

The intellect and the emotions are also part of the ego. These parts of our ego can be very dangerous in relation to Karma; here are a couple of examples:

For many years I worked as a doorman at various night-clubs, during these years my ego grew and grew. This is always the danger when we believe that we hold a position of status, of power. I believed I was pretty good at my job. I also practiced the Martial Arts from a very young age.

Eventually at the age of 26, I outgrew this line of employment, in step with my increasing search for spiritual truth, but continued with my Martial Arts.

Without going into detail, I was violently assaulted at the age of 44yrs old by a 22yr old. We had a family get together as one member of the family was going into a war zone imminently. The drinking got out of hand; when the unprovoked assault happened I was defenceless as I was very drunk and in a comatose sleep.

The following day I was enraged and felt humiliated, my first thought was revenge, "that person would not have been able to do that to me under equal circumstances". I was in an emotional and mental hurricane; I also went into bouts of depression.

The immense power of the ego can be seen at work here. "How can this all be Maya, illusion, the lumps, bumps, bruising, and blood were very real? How can this happen to me? Where is the justice in this"? I was on an emotional roller coaster.

"I am not putting up with that. I can't believe what he did to me and in my own home." *I/me/mine = ego*. The assault was me beating me up (the reality is that at some point when working as a doorman I had dished out a beating), nothing less than a Karmic payback…it was very, very, incredibly hard to swallow, almost impossibly so…I felt crushed.

Teachings from my mentor slowly began to filter into my consciousness. "You know you cannot go seeking revenge, it would create terrible Karma".

The perpetrator of the attack may have done so on the spur of the moment, yet still created unskilful Karma for himself.

But here was "I", planning a full-blown assault, planned with *intent*. All I would succeed in doing would be to set myself up for another visitation of terrible unskilful Karma. Yes, we all have a right to defend our bodies, but in this case, I was unable to, it was my Karma, and it was paid back as unpalatable as it was at the time.

My master had informed me that there is also what is known as the law of nine. The further you progress up the mountain, the more aware you become of these laws, consequently the visitation of unskilfully created Karma increases on a sliding scale of 1 to 9.

The repercussions if I went ahead with a revenge mission would go far deeper than the initial parties involved in the foregoing example; let's say it was my partner's son who made the initial assault and I then carry out revenge on him.

The shock and horror that would be visited upon his mother would be dreadful. The despair that my partner would suffer, knowing that by my actions I had just terminated our relationship. Then there would be the shock and horror that would be visited upon his grandparents. Also what of the shock and horror that would descend upon her son's partner and young child? What if he sustained terrible injury and could no longer provide for his family? All of these ramifications would be visited back upon me in time and that on the sliding scale of one to nine.

And so the shock waves continue outward, like waves and ripples on a pond caused by a stone, and the name of this stone is ego.

So here we can see how a vicious cycle can be set up. This kind of cycle can be created in a multitude of ways, on an hourly/daily/yearly basis through thoughts, words, and deeds. This can build up to such a level, that we have no other choice but to reincarnate again and again and again.

These white-water rapids that were breaking me up, created by my own ego, were on the verge of throwing me off my life raft of spiritual practice. I was on the verge of throwing the towel in; ready to dismiss spiritual truth as utter nonsense in order to give myself the green light to repair my damaged ego. But by keeping hold of my spiritual practice I eventually came to the realisation that this incident was down to my Karma, Karma that was created during my nine years as a doorman.

All of us should try to break this chain of events, hence Jesus the Christ saying, "Turn the other cheek". It means we need to be very, very careful with our responses.

The ego will hang on frantically to anything that means its survival; the ego will even lead you to your death if you allow it to, just so it can incarnate again.

As Deus had said, a slight bend in the mind can turn into a major warp; on the final great path ego pursuits will become magnified. Of course it took this event to awaken me to what was really going on.

Most of what made up the identity of the fully-fledged ego personality all those years ago, prior to striving for the truth, needed to be dismantled.

The ego had lead me into believing a few beers are all right, which of course anything in moderation is ok, sex is sex, but a dirty mouth (carries intent) is something else, so avoid extremes, moderation and balance are the key words.

In ancient Chinese culture balance is expressed by the symbol of the Yin and Yang symbol. To follow the Tao (pronounced Dow), which means the way, and is much the same as the Asian Dharma, is to live by the principle of Yin and Yang, to maintain a balance in life. This is the underlying principle of the Kabbalistic Tree of Life – balance.

Pain often accompanies a new beginning, what seemed to be happening was that my karma was being paid off in equal measure to my aspiration, for, in order to step off of the wheel of rebirth all Karma has to be paid back. This is why it takes great courage to press on. The truth is, the higher up the mountain you climb, the harder the path becomes.

Another, far subtler manifestation of the ego happened as I was reviewing this chapter on ego. I had parked up my car at the gym. As I shut the car door I saw some leaflets on the back seat I was to pass on to a friend. So, I opened the rear door to retrieve them – the door wouldn't shut. A long story short, the mechanic, despite me fervently offering up prayers, couldn't fix it so had to tie the door shut with some cord. Driving home, I felt extremely stressed with the whole situation, then a car pulled in front of me. This car's personal registration was J9 EGO. I recalled being upset a long time ago and the words from Deuce, 'Which part of you is upset?' The answer was the ego, inwardly I laughed; and, of course, I had been told, nothing happens by accident.

The ego's struggle for control will increase as we get nearer to the top of the mountain, but when we finally reach the summit, the new person is born. The process is very much like a grub (ego) transforming into a chrysalis (withdrawing from the world) and finally bursting forth as its true self – a beautiful butterfly.

We can now see what good our ego's do for us...absolutely nothing. Good thoughts words and deeds, done without ego, done without thought for reward, hourly/ weekly/ monthly/ yearly, will gradually build up that bank of skilful Karma, which by this law has to come back.

This karmic law was described by the Master thus: If you imagine yourself sitting in water, you pull the water towards yourself with both hands. As fast as you pull the water in, even quicker does the water move away from you, exiting from both sides of your body. If conversely you push the water away from yourself, the quicker the water returns to you from both sides.

Love, devotion, giving, and compassion will weaken the ego; it will eventually lead us to the ultimate, "Moksha" and liberation.

Although the above example is a rather intense one, the ego can be far subtler; there will be many highs and many lows, as the ego strains to keep a hold.

"Why doesn't anything happen when I meditate? Oh this is all a waste of time and energy. Why do I not see beautiful visions? Why can't I travel in the body of light? I am told of all these things but, but, but". All of this belongs to the ego. As the Avatar Mother Meera says: Visions may come, visions may go, but the silence always remains.

This silence is not an external silence, it represents the silencing of the mind from all thoughts in meditation. This silencing of the mind brings into play, in due course, the changing of brain waves; Beta to Alpha, Alpha to Theta and so on.

The power of this truth – silence – unites all of humanity; with silence there is no theological or philosophical concepts that cause division. All faiths, all beliefs, unite at the top of the mountain in silence, a silence that is just pure consciousness...there is absolutely no division, no divisiveness in pure silence, a silence that is a shared consciousness of "Am-ness"; the foundation of which is love; a pure oneness.

And so, it comes to pass that your ego has created for you your personality traits, traits that make you what you are. At death you will pass over to the astral; the astral has many mansions, many different parts.

Dependent upon what has gone to make up what you believe to be you, to *that part* of the astral will you go. "Birds of a feather flock together".

Loving and giving entities will all go to that part of the astral set aside for such entities, thieves, robbers, murderers, the violent etc. will all go to that part of the astral set aside for them, not a very pleasant place to be.

They who sanction and they who carry out mass murder and torture, will suffer every one of those deaths. As soon as a murder is committed, the murderer has to be reincarnated again, to be murdered.

The ego is incredibly difficult to deal with, but to deal with the ego through love; through love of the Divine; through love of humanity; for love of the planet; to turn your attention away from yourself towards the needs of others will help. By this approach you are in effect putting the ego on a diet.

It is never too late to step upon the path of transformation, to start to create a more loving and brighter future for yourself, and for others.

177

CHAPTER 17

FUNDAMENTAL LAWS OF THE UNIVERSE

All the laws are an expression of the ONE DIVINE GOD.

The entire universe is made up of energy, these are the basic building blocks of all creation:

Energy is always changing; it cannot be created or destroyed e.g. firewood – ash; water – ice; seed – acorn – tree. Your big toe is made up of the same energy/atoms as the stars; it's just arranged in a different way.

All things are relative, e.g. if you sprained your wrist it would not be as bad as fracturing your wrist.

The law of vibration. Everything in the universe vibrates; everything is in a state of motion, a state of flux. Mud, you, the car, is all vibrations (seemingly separate but in reality this is Maya). Love is the most powerful energy in the universe.

The law of polarity. Everything has an opposite. North – South, hot –cold, love – hate. White and black are different poles of colour, big and small are poles of one and the same thing, size. All are different degrees of the one.

The law of rhythm. High tide – low tide; side to side; up and down; everything flows to the law of rhythm...SPIRIT INTO MATTER = TIME – MATTER INTO SPIRIT.

The law of cause and effect. Karma; what goes around comes around whether skilful or unskilful. You must learn that INTENT is the pivotal point.

The law of gender/creation. WOMAN = FEMININE = IDEAS – MAN = DOING. There must be a male and a female to form a new creation. Protons have a positive charge, Electrons have a negative charge.

What can we say with respect to time? If it were not for time, all would happen at once and we as human beings would miss it all.

The seven colours

All colours vibrate; each has its own unique vibration and property. They are as follows:

RED – Stimulating
ORANGE – Vitalizing
YELLOW – Quickening
GREEN – Harmonizing
BLUE – Peace inducing and pain relieving
INDIGO – Purifying
VIOLET – Silencing

These correspond to the seven chakras (pronounced shakras), which we will go into in further detail shortly. Other colours we wish to add to this list are:

WHITE – Regenerating
BLACK – Strengthening
GREY – Neutralizing
ROSE PINK – Soothing
BROWN – Stabilizing

All of these come from the one source for our use. We can use these colours in colour meditation e.g. if you were feeling tired you may wish to use the colour red.

Adopting our body posture, mudra etc. imagine you are surrounded by the colour, imagine it to be a mist, or light, you imagine you are breathing the colour in and out.

Gradually you imagine the colour to permeate every cell and every atom of your being, eventually there is only this colour and nothing else exists.

With respect to the corresponding colours for the chakras, always proceed up the scale, starting with red.

If for example you wanted to work with the colour blue, you would precede red, orange, yellow, green, then arrive at the colour blue, meditating on that chosen colour for the remainder of your meditation.

Science already acknowledges that all colours vibrate at different rates and can have a beneficial effect upon the individual's wellbeing.

There is an illness called SAD (seasonal associated disorder). This is treated by gazing at an ultra violet light.

I was confided in by a friend that she suffered from this illness; I gave her the colour meditation of violet. A grateful phone call was soon received, not only that, but she had passed the practice on to others with the same disorder producing encouraging results.

This world's apparent reality manifests through certain mediums of the human form, in the first instance via the brain and the five senses. However there are other mechanisms at work on a subtler level.

Chakras

There are seven Chakras (wheels), six are within the human body, and one outside located just above the crown of the head.

Each Chakra as it becomes active spins in a flipping motion, imagine a pin running through and across its circular diameter, it acts as a valve so to speak. Most people have only the first couple of chakras open.

There are various practices and forms of meditation which will open these Chakras; Kundalini Yoga is one such practice. In Tantric Yoga; their aim is to awaken the Kundalini force, which is located at the base of the spine.

Kundalini is known as the serpent force and is represented as a hooded cobra in many cultures. It is represented in Egyptian iconography as a cobra coming from the Ajna Chakra, located in the forehead. The Egyptian headdress (believed to represent a Lion's mane), along with the plated beard, also represents the Hooded Cobra.

When the Kundalini force rises and pierces the six internal Chakras it opens up what is known as the third eye. In Ancient Egypt; the foundation for the western mystery tradition, the third eye was represented by the eye of Horus or the all Seeing Eye of Freemasonry; in the eastern tradition, that of India, it is represented by the eye of Shiva.

Unless you are under the direct guidance of a master, avoid practices that are said to work directly on the Chakras or directly to awaken Kundalini. Mental institutes around the world are full of people who have come unstuck with such practices. The best way to explain the danger would be to liken plugging in a 100watt bulb, into a 1,000,000 watt current.

It is prudent here to mention the practice of Pranayama. Pranayama is a yogic practice in controlling the breath.

This is done by placing the middle finger of the right hand, at the Ajna Chakra, the thumb then closes the right nostril; breathe in through the left nostril. On

181

completing the breath hold for three seconds. This nostril controls the flow of what is known as the channel of Ida.

Next close the left nostril with the third finger, releasing the thumb from the right nostril, breathe out through the right nostril (the right nostril controls the flow of the channel of Pingala), on completion hold for three seconds.

Next breathe in through the right nostril, hold for three, close the right nostril, and breathe out through the left. This completes one cycle. Warning! Do not attempt to do more than eight cycles.

There are three channels that run up the spine, Ida starts on the left, Pingala on the right and spiral from right to left as they rise through the chakras up the spine; Sushumna is fixed in the centre. The Greek symbol of the winged caduceus, used in the medical profession, represents Ida, Pingala and Sushumna.

At any one time during the day we only breathe in and out through one nostril, it will alternate from right to left periodically.

If Pranayama is overdone, it will cause the channel of Sushumna to open, allowing the Kundalini power that is dormant at the base of the spine to awaken, it will then surge up the spine through the Chakras before the aspirant is ready.

Any practice of Pranayama other than that given above should be avoided.

As mentioned, the path of the Bhakti Yogi is a safe path. As we proceed with our Sadhana, our spiritual practice, the Chakras are worked on by the Divine.

Each one in succession is gradually and very carefully opened. Rather than forcing Kundalini up the chakras to an unprepared mind, which would be disastrous, what is actually happening is the complete human being, mind, body and spirit, are being worked on by the Divine.

As you continue with meditation, you may start to feel and experience strange sensations in and around the body. You may feel a tingling or butterfly like sensation in the forehead or you may experience tingling or an undulating, and sometimes both sensations going up the spine. Sometimes you may experience an involuntary shake/twisting of the torso.

At any time, you may experience what feels like a mist or magnetic field around the head, it is quite a blissful sensation. It reminds me of a halo that you see in Christian iconography; this is the omnipotent Divine presence. It is Divine light entering the body in most of these cases.

With respect to the spinal sensations, in some cases, but not all, it is the Kundalini force starting to rise through the channel of Sushumna, and through the chakras. Some sensations may be localized at various points along the spine; this is when a particular chakra is being worked on by the Divine.

In some cases, as a direct result of your spiritual practice, you will attain to what is known as siddhi powers. There are quite a few different siddhi powers, such as being able to move objects, seeing into the future, reading the minds of others etc.

If this does happen to you, it is best to thank the Divine, thank God etc. for bestowing it upon you, but graciously turn it down by offering it back.

The reason for not using these powers is an extremely important one. Firstly it would distract you from your mission of attaining Moksha. Secondly the biggest danger is that the ego will seize upon the power. Before you know it the life raft of your Sadhana, your spiritual practice, will be dashed upon rocks in the rapids of Karmic payback. The ego will grow and whisper in your mind. "Look I can do this, I can do that."

If you are following the path of the Bhakti Yogi, do not let these sensations worry you. If at any time you do feel concern, then stop your practice and seek advice from a master.

CHAPTER 18

MAINSTREAM YOGA

There are many, many forms of yoga; it is outside of the scope of this book to cover them all. What we will do is to give a brief description of what is considered to be the core practices.

Rajah Yoga

The core of Raja Yoga is the eight limbs of Yoga as given by Patanjali, its primary objective is to connect the practitioner with their Soul, which is located as mentioned before, between the eyebrows in the centre of the forehead.

Raja Yoga employs various meditative techniques to accomplish this, one of which is called Tractcatum.

Tractcatum is performed by staring at the flame of a candle for a few moments, then closing the eyes to focus upon the image of the flame left in the middle of the forehead, upon the screen of your mind. The aim of Tractcatum is to hone the concentration and focus.

Again, caution should be taken in performing this practice. A qualified teacher should be sought. Watch out for the ego here, "Oh I will be all right without a teacher". No you won't. If you are following the path of Bhakti, of love and devotion, ask and pray for continued protection in your quest for self-realization, providing you are sincere, it will be there.

Another objective of Rajah Yoga is the control of the mind, its thoughts and habits. Our everyday thoughts and actions are known as sanskars in Rajah Yoga. Our habits are likened to a horse and cart being driven along a track over and over again. So given time the ruts or furrows created become ever deeper, thus making it harder to correct. Rajah Yoga seeks to eliminate negative traits, replacing them with positive traits.

Bhakti Yoga

As formerly described, is the path of love and devotion, love and devotion to your chosen deity to the Divine, to God; love and devotion to humanity; love and devotion to your family etc. It is centred within the heart.

Karma Yoga

Karma yoga is based on right action. A karma yoga practitioner will endeavour to create positive karma in thought, word and deed. Most people involved in karma yoga are vegetarian, avoiding harming any living being, including insects.
　　The main issue, which has been largely over looked through the millennia, is INTENT, the pivotal point of good or bad Karma.

Jnana Yoga

Jnana yoga is the yoga of right knowledge, it is the study of sacred scripture, it is the study of nature and it's the Dharana (contemplation), of life and the human condition in order to arrive at the truth. The Jnana yogi sees all as the Divine. When finally seeing through the appearance of things, that all is one, this is known as Sahaja.

Wisdom note:

'You are all caskets of Divine Love; share it, spread it. Express that Love in acts of service, words of sympathy, thoughts of compassion. Just as when you awake from sleep, you know that the dream which you had was a matter of minutes, though the chain of events dreamt spanned many years, this life will appear a transient affair when you awake into *Jnana* (wisdom) after this brief "dream of life." Be always full of joy so that when your time is up, you can quit with a light laugh, and not whimper in grief. So shape your lives and activities such that this supreme joy will be your lasting possession.' Sai Baba

Hatha Yoga

Hatha yoga (Ha = sun, Tha = moon), fundamentally is to do with keeping a healthy body, and healthy mind.

It not only seeks to keep muscles firm and flexible, it also seeks through its various asanas (postures), to massage and keep aligned all the internal organs. It also works on what is called the Nadis, various energy centres and channels running throughout the body, similar to the acupuncture meridians in Chinese medicine.

By working on the spine and Nadis, it balances the body in preparation for the rise of kundalini.

Wisdom note:

'The body is the temple of God; in every body, God is installed, whether the owner of the body recognizes it or not. It is God that inspires you to good acts, that warns you against the bad. Listen to that Voice. Obey that Voice and you will not come to any harm. A lady wept that her necklace was lost or stolen; she searched everywhere and became inconsolably sad. Then, when she passed across a mirror, she found the lost necklace around her neck. It was there all the time. Similarly, God is there, as the Inner Dweller whether you know it or not.' Sai Baba

Kundalini Yoga

Kundalini yoga seeks to awaken the serpent force at the base of the spine.

Once awake, it surges up the channel of Sushumna and through the chakras to unite with the seventh and last chakra, in order to attain enlightenment.

As stated earlier, a very dangerous practice, unless carried out under the instruction of a true master, of which there are very few in the world. We strongly advise against this practice for, as mentioned earlier, to awaken Kundalini before the aspirant is ready is akin to plugging a 100watt bulb into a 1,000,000watt current.

In reality, the teaching which is laid out here constitutes an amalgam of the above mainstream yoga's, it comes together to form a very powerful practice.

We do not have a name in a religious sense, we do respect all religion, and yes religions can form a very good foundation for advancement.

What we aspire to is completeness, rather than say we are this, or we are that, we just say we are spiritual.

One last thing before signing off, for most it will be difficult to incorporate all of the foregoing into your life all at once. I would suggest you re-read this a few times to get a feel for the Final Great Path. Then create a plan, perhaps even draw up a Gant chart, similar to that used in the building trade to map a building site's progression.

Start off, say with a meditation once a week for a month, then increase to twice a week and so on. Eventually add other practices to your Sadhana, until eventually, in a year or two, you find you have comfortably assimilated the whole practice as laid out. The most important thing here is to enjoy, do not see it as a chore. There are no flags that will pop up to say yes you have achieved. The test is over time, when you can look back over a number of years and see, recognise you have become a different person. True signs of progress is a calmer and more compassionate nature, one that is loving and caring – this path is one of gentle transformation.

Remember, you have free will and can step off the path at any time, never is a step on this path ever lost.

Wisdom note:

'The king is honoured only inside his Kingdom; he is adored only within its borders. But the virtuous man is honoured and adored in all countries. A person may have outstanding physical beauty; he may have the sparkle of robust youth; he may boast of a high noble lineage; he may be a famed scholar. But, if he lacks the virtues that spiritual discipline can ensure, he is to be reckoned only as a beautiful flower, with no fragrance.' Sai Baba

Many a time Deus would just reply to my unspoken thoughts before they had a chance to manifest, for example on this particular occasion. I had written version one of this book; it didn't include the western approach to re-merging with the Divine. It had been on my mind for quite some time, should I disclose the aspect of the Great Pyramid and Tree of Life? Finally I decided to ask the Master directly. 'Deus, should I reveal...'

'Yes! Elucidate the western approach please.' Came the interrupted reply to my recurring unexpressed thoughts.

THE FINAL GREAT PATH

Summary

Following my introduction to Avatars, a slow distillation process took place in guiding me into a form of Bhakti Yoga; this yogic practice is the path of "Love and Devotion".

Love and devotion is the foundation for all exoteric religions. For me, the path of Bhakti began a healing and redemptive process, but it was much, much more than that.

The Final Great Path places the onus for progression squarely on the shoulders of the aspirant. It is incumbent upon the striving devotee to put the work in, to move ever closer to the Divine...*take just one step towards the Divine and the Divine will take one-hundred steps towards you.* The Final Great Path is not passive, it is emphatically active; it is a process of magnetising the descent of Divine Light and grace.

It is almost impossible for me to relate the simple beauty and truth of the Master's teachings, but the most poignant aspect was having a personal relationship with a real-deal spiritual "Master".

Many spiritual scriptures are truly wonderful, but you can't ask a book questions for clarification; or just simply ask a book any old question for that matter and expect an answer.

Let's take the subject of Karma as an example, the general belief in Karma, whenever it is mentioned, is in a negative context. 'Poor old John, that tree that fell on his head must have been his Karma.' How many times do we hear this negative association with Karma? The rendition I got from Deus was enlightening.

First of all he told me that Karma is non conditional, it is automatic; there is no supreme being casting judgement on our deeds. Karma is also both positive and negative, it acts like a spiritual bank. So if you continue to do good deeds you will get good back; so you don't always get a tree fall on your head.

But the most important thing about Karma is what he called the pivotal point. This pivotal point is "Intent", and is rarely mentioned in scripture if at all. If you "intend" an action (which includes verbal), you incur Karma, positive or negative. Without intent the Karma is neutral.

This collective all-encompassing explanation of Karma explained much that had come to pass in my life.

Over many years Deus had imparted his teachings to David, the Founder of Zenyogkido and founder member of the British Wheel of Yoga. These teachings were, under the Master's direction, skilfully woven within his martial art. The teaching of Karma is the foundation of the jewel of right conduct. My asking of many questions relating to spiritual matters I found to be the foundation for the Jewel of Right Knowledge; right knowledge is Jnana Yoga. This of course brings me to that of Right Belief, to believe in God, the Divine, in Avatars. To be active in your devotion; not just paying lip service. To truly love the Divine, to be ever mindful of the Divine; this is Bhakti Yoga...the devotional path.

This mindfulness brings in the process of watching your thoughts, for thoughts manifest into the outer world. The chair you sit on once started off as a thought.

If your thoughts are dark they lead you into a dark place – the opposite is true of thoughts filled with light and peace. This training of the mind comes under Raja Yoga; the Royal Path.

With respect to Ha Tha Yoga (Ha = Sun, Tha = Moon), unifying the body with the breath in order to keep it fit and healthy; the physical side of Zenyogkido does the same.

So hidden within the spiritual Yin side of Zenyogkido is Ha Tha Yoga; Karma Yoga; Jnana Yoga; Raja Yoga and Bhakti Yoga – all unified under the one umbrella..."The Way of the Mind, Body and Spirit.

In due course, Deus had imparted to David the three elemental keys for progression, Focus, Affirmation and Aspiration. Applied martially the "focus" could be the black belt, you "aspire" too and that through your training you "affirm" you will be a black belt 1st Degree. For this you need "faith", a belief that you will attain your goal. Doubt is the opposite pole of faith. If you focus on doubt it grows bigger and bigger and is very destructive...you attain nothing but darkness. Focus on faith and it grows, everything becomes attainable.

Spiritually, your focus is upon the Divine, you aspire to become self and God realised through your practice and you affirm that you are one with the Divine. My teacher, Deus, once said to me, 'Jim, faith is the bridge between the shore of uncertainty and the shore of certainty.'

This gradual immersion into the Divine from your focus, begins to grow. Deus frequently advised to give just a little time to the Divine each day, he used the analogy of a pie chart – just give a small segment to your Divine-self, your real self, each and every day.

Gently and gradually Deus introduced me to prayer, of course I was familiar with this from my time within the Catholic Church. But rather than the usual formula of the "Our Father" officially known as the "Lord's Prayer" and the "Hail Mary", Deus educated me in being a little more thoughtful about prayer.

Prayer, he said, connects us directly with the Divine, so be careful what you ask for.

Through careful consideration and from the finger that points the way I refined my prayers. 'Each day Jim, pray for world peace.' Deus advised. In due course I produced what I considered to be a very meaningful Divine request. 'Dear Lord, please bring lasting peace and harmony between all nations, all cultures all creeds and all religions; may mutual respect, understanding and harmony prevail amongst all.'

Included within my daily prayers is: 'Please bring balance and harmony back to Mother Nature, the human race and your creation in general.' 'Dear Lord I ask and pray for the good health and wellbeing of the following' – then list...

Daily requests are also made for my own spiritual progression, not just for me but for the sake of the world. What I mean by for the sake of the world, is just to have a positive impact for the good in my day to day interactions. The most important aspect to prayer is that it should be heart-felt.

At the right time Deus also introduced me to Jappa Mantra. Mantra is the repetition of Divine words/sound. That which qualifies mantra as Divine is at once its vibrational rate and the fact it connects you, once again, directly to the Divine. Cymatics is the science of the effects of sound on the material and proves that sound has a profound effect upon everything.

Mantra can be either vocalised or repeated mentally within. The beauty of doing mantra is that it leaves no room in the mind for stray thoughts (which can be negative in content), and immediately connects you to the Divine. Mantra can be done at any time of the day or night. In fact as soon as my head hits the pillow, I do Jappa Mantra until I fall asleep. Adding to my bed-time mantra, I ask and pray for my spiritual practice to continue into the sleeping state.

You may have got the picture by now, what was in the beginning of this amazing path, just a small segment of the pie chart, gradually grew exponentially. The spiritual focus just grows in light, like the sun at sunrise, increasing your immersion into the Divine. Condensing his teachings, Deus imparted these fundamentals:

Focus
Affirmation
Aspiration
Jappa Mantra
Prayer
Meditation

The amazing thing about this immersion, is that outwardly nobody knows, it's not glitzy or showy; externally you are no different to anyone else.

191

The world can seem a very complicated place, which it is at present. Worldwide the view of law and order is just so diverse. Contravening law and order embraces justice. But the global perspective of justice is again so very diverse.

An amazingly simple tool was provided to me by Deus as a litmus test for everyday interaction with people... "Deserve – Don't deserve".

That of human rights is an interesting example. We talk about the human rights of those serving a prison sentence but using deserve – don't deserve as the litmus test, those guilty of breaching the human rights of the "law abiding" citizen, lose their own human rights, simple. Deserve/don't deserve can be levelled at any awkward life situation.

My education in walking the final great path continued, another important aspect to this path is – "keeping the right company". The old cliché of birds of a feather flock together is true, it goes under the law of magnetism.

If a person full of virtue begins to mix with the unvirtuous, that virtue will be compromised and at some point lost. However, the same can be said of the opposite. The person without morals and virtues, if they break away from bad company and begin to mix with good; their conscience can be stirred into change; virtue can be grown.

Returning once again to one of the "major keys" that of *Focus*, using the analogy of a garden. If one were to focus on creating a beautiful garden, with focus, affirmation and aspiration the beautiful garden, "with hard work", would soon become a reality. However, if our focus were to be removed from sustaining the garden, in a short space of time, weeds would appear and the garden would become overgrown; before long the beautiful garden would disappear.

I remember when I took my first steps along this spiritual path, it was easy, interesting, so much to learn. The promises of peace, contentment and wonderful spiritual experiences...even gaining power over whatever this world could throw at me was alluring, and yet the reality of this latter aspect is totally, "impossible". Yes, the early stages are pleasant, just like when first starting to climb a mountain; but like a mountain, it gets harder and harder the higher you climb.

Spiritual experiences may or may not come as the path is unique to each and every one. The hunt for spiritual experiences can become a trap in itself, to clarify this position I here quote what Mother Meera has to say on the subject. 'Visons may come and visions may go, but the silence always remains.'

This path, this journey, I tell you now, is not for the faint hearted; it is not a sprint, in fact it is the toughest marathon you could ever wish to run – a lifetime in duration. You will be faced in due course with all of your frailties, all of your negatives, all of the flaws in your character. Furthermore, the flaws that we refuse to address just get magnified to the point of distress. All of these trials and tribulations are linked to the ego and the ego is very cunning, so much so, it will even lead you to your death in order for it to reincarnate again. The internationally renowned martial artist and self-help guru, Geoff Thompson, calls this, the dark and destructive part of our being, the "shadow self". The ego does not want to die, so over many years Deus delicately changed my thought processes through modification, leading me away from being egocentric. Don't get me wrong here, I'm most certainly not Mr Perfect, my ego does flare up every now and then – we just have to keep a constant vigil over it.

On this life's journey, I hungered to be a warrior, someone to be respected. But in my youth I was misguided, I had a distorted perception of what life is all about. To be fair, this distorted perception wasn't just about my personal ignorance, I was also a product of my surroundings. I was conditioned by people who were equally ignorant.

What I have found, in the decades after quitting the doors (night club security), is that the ultimate warrior has nothing to do with physical prowess. The real warrior is the person who sets out on the spiritual quest; the quest to conquer the self; whilst juggling with the daily battle of so-called mundane life. This battle is looking after your loved ones, your family; holding down the nine-to-five job, whilst balancing it with that quest for the spiritual Holy Grail…that is true courage.

I'm now 60 years young at the time of writing and have an advantage over much younger people, in that I can reflect upon a pretty interesting life's journey to date.

As children we are, generally speaking, bewildered by the vastness and uncertainty of the world; adults are giants, garden walls and fences are massive fortifications. The playgrounds at school and fields we play in are vast expanses. We move, with age, from school to school, at first looking up to our elder students as really mature and aspiring to be like them. Yet eventually we become that mature student, walls and fences become playthings; the vast expanses becoming smaller.

The hormones kick in throughout our teens, nothing else matters other than the opposite sex. Like adolescent lions, we challenge the status quo, vying for position. Before we know it, in our twenties we have settled down from sewing our wild oats and are involved in family life and the responsibility it brings. We have now become the adult giants.

From thirty we start to become aware of the aging process and our perspective on life begins to change – slowly. We watch our children grow up, going through the same processes – then grand-children, time seems to go so much quicker and we ask ourselves, "What's going on?" At this point we become somewhat more reflective on life, some try to put a positive slant on things, "family is everything". Others can become depressed with advancing age. The older we get, we become either more reflective and adjust to a more spiritually contemplative way of life, or eventually implode.

Life is divided into phases, with age one should naturally gravitate and evolve spiritually – nothing forced, just a gradual progression. There is a need, at some point, to realize our minute individual human insignificance, we are not giants, and yet we are very much more than human, we need to wake up to our own very real spiritual significance. If you believe you are only human, then that's all you will be.

The ancient mystery tradition followed and explained this division of life; these phases, by using the natural astrophysical course of the sun. Sunrise, as that of birth and childhood, rising in due course to its Zenith and the full power of maturity. From thence its downward trajectory to its death, the setting sun; where we have gained spiritual knowledge and wisdom to take with us on the next phase of our journey.

Often I have contemplated what my life would have been like without this spiritual search; without that faith in a greater reality and a supreme being. As I ponder that question, all I can see is darkness, anxiety and despair for those who deny this possibility. Denying that possibility is to rob your life of any kind of meaning or purpose.

Within the confines of the body, our five senses report information to the brain, but our five senses are limited; they don't and can't deliver the full picture. There are sounds we cannot hear, colours we cannot see, scents we cannot smell, tastes we cannot savour; our perception of reality is only partial.

Putting the philosophical side of things to one side though, just on an experiential footing, I have been privileged to actually live opposite poles of being. Rather than buying into just one perspective, I've focused and chased down a broad cross section of relative realities. What I have found is not necessarily spiritual truth, but that..."The Truth is Spiritual"; we are spiritual beings on a material journey, not material beings on a spiritual journey. In the western esoteric tradition, this pursuit of the truth is known as "The Great Work". For me, my work is not yet done, there is still much to do...I am not an Avatar and although striving to be, I'm not an Avadhutta either (Self Realised), but I know the path I've taken is going in the right direction.

Do not be in haste for the absolute, ask yourself, am I duly and truly prepared for moksha/self-realisation? What would happen to your mind/psyche at present, if when washing your face you suddenly realised you were washing yourself with yourself?

THE FINAL GREAT PATH

Be patient and have faith – either in this life or the next you will commune with the Divine…God speed, Love to you.

If you have enjoyed The Final Great Path – East and feel this knowledge would benefit the world, please feel free to visit Amazon and place a review. God bless.

THE FINAL GREAT PATH

Printed in Great Britain
by Amazon

43101422R00110